MONTESSORI INCLUSION

STRATEGIES AND STORIES OF SUPPORT FOR LEARNERS WITH EXCEPTIONALITIES

ANN EPSTEIN, PhD
EDITOR

WITH NATALIE DANNER, PhD
FOREWORD BY AMIRA MOGAJI

A division of Montessori Services
Santa Rosa, CA

www.montessoriservices.com

Copyright © 2020 Ann Epstein, Primary Editor

Chapter 1 – *Better Together: Montessori & Special Education*
  © 2020 Brian J. Berger and Dena J. AuCoin

Chapter 2 – *What New (and Not So New) Montessori Teachers Need to Know About Special Education*
  © 2020 Andrée Rolfe

Chapter 3 – *Following All the Children: A Montessori Model of Tiered Instruction*
  © 2020 Jacqueline Cossentino and Elizabeth G. Slade

Chapter 4 – *An Overview of a Montessori-Based Multi-Tiered System of Support*
  © 2020 Christine Lowry

Chapter 5 – *Supporting Children with Exceptionalities in an Independent Montessori School*
  © 2020 Paul Epstein and Diane Betzolt

Chapter 6 – *How Can I Tell Her Parents?*
  © 2020 Cathie Perolman

Chapter 7 – *Montessori Teacher Supports for Children with Exceptionalities*
  © 2020 Ann Epstein

Chapter 8 – *Montessori as a Safe Haven for Childhood Trauma*
  © 2020 Maria Eva Chaffin and Brynn Rangel

Chapter 9 – Trauma-Informed Montessori
  © 2020 Colleen Wilkinson

Chapter 10 – *Including Young Children with Severe Disabilities in Raintree Montessori School: The Circle of Inclusion* © 2020 Barbara Thompson and Pamela Shanks

Chapter 11 – *Elizabeth Academy: Awakening to a New Dawn*
  © 2020 Gail Williamsen with Lizzie Dalton and Mandy Fuhriman

All rights reserved. No part of this book may be used or reproduced in any manner whatsoever without written permission except in the case of brief quotations embedded in critical articles and reviews.

ISBN# 978-0-939195-59-6 (Paperback Edition)
ISBN# 978-0-939195-65-7 (eBook Edition)
Library of Congress Control Number 2020932807

Cover Design by Kristie Jade Woods
Book Design by Shannon McMath

Printed in Korea
First Printing 2020

A division of Montessori Services
Santa Rosa, CA
www.montessoriservices.com

IN REMEMBRANCE OF
JACQUELINE COSSENTINO, PhD

With sincere gratitude, we dedicate this book to our colleague and friend, Dr. Jacqueline Cossentino (1964–2019). We celebrate her many contributions to the Montessori community. She was a nexus, focused on connecting Montessorians with research outcomes, important initiatives, and exciting new ideas. Children—particularly those attending public Montessori schools—were at the heart of Jackie's work. She tackled the complex issue of assessment with diligent research, creativity, and practicality. She worked to develop the practice of child study to respond to the individual needs of children in a developmentally healthy way. Those of us who had the pleasure of working directly with Jackie marveled at her ability to light up a room with an ever-present enthusiasm and a "can-do" approach to challenges. Jackie's body of work, along with her intelligence, caring heart, and infectious humor, strengthened the Montessori community and has made the rest of us better equipped to serve all children.

TABLE OF CONTENTS

Foreword — Amira Mogaji vi

Preface — Natalie Danner ix

Introduction — Ann Epstein xi

Montessori & Special Education

Chapter 1 1
Better Together: Montessori & Special Education
Brian J. Berger and Dena J. AuCoin

Chapter 2 14
What New (and Not So New) Montessori Teachers Need to Know About Special Education
Andrée Rolfe

Current Procedures & Supports

Chapter 3 29
Following All the Children: A Montessori Model of Tiered Instruction
Jacqueline Cossentino and Elizabeth G. Slade

Chapter 4 44
An Overview of a Montessori-Based Multi-Tiered System of Support
Christine Lowry

Chapter 5 51
Supporting Children with Exceptionalities in an Independent Montessori School
Paul Epstein and Diane Betzolt

TABLE OF CONTENTS

Chapter 6 69
How Can I Tell Her Parents?
Cathie Perolman

Chapter 7 87
Montessori Teacher Supports for Children with Exceptionalities
Ann Epstein

Chapter 8 101
Montessori as a Safe Haven for Childhood Trauma
Maria Eva Chaffin and Brynn Rangel

Chapter 9 110
Trauma-Informed Montessori
Colleen Wilkinson

Fully Inclusive Schools

Chapter 10. 118
Including Young Children with Severe Disabilities in Raintree Montessori School: The Circle of Inclusion
Barbara Thompson and Pamela Shanks

Chapter 11. 140
Elizabeth Academy: Awakening to a New Dawn
Gail Williamsen with Lizzie Dalton and Mandy Fuhriman

References 157

Acknowledgments 179

FOREWORD

According to the National Council of Disability (2018), segregation of students from non-disabled peers occurs and is dictated by "the zip code in which they live, their race, and disability label" (p. 9). The Individuals with Disabilities Education Act states:

> Disability is a natural part of the human experience and in no way diminishes the right of individuals to participate in or contribute to society. Improving educational results for children with disabilities is an essential element of our national policy of ensuring equality of opportunity, full participation, independent living, and economic self-sufficiency for individuals with disabilities. (U. S. Department of Education, 2019)

So what is the solution? How do we live up to the promises we made as we were completing our Montessori training, when we believed that every child can benefit from a Montessori education? With inclusive practices, the Montessori guide has the power to meet more of the needs of children they serve and allow students to grow and thrive. In this book, inclusive practices for children with exceptionalities are explained and demystified.

Over 100 years ago, Dr. Maria Montessori advised us to "follow the child." We currently live in a time when it seems like humanity does not prioritize children's rights. At the United States border, infants and children are being traumatized, separated from their families, and imprisoned without even the most basic necessities. Racism is inextricably linked to poor academic outcomes for Black children and is now considered an Adverse Childhood Experience (ACE) by many educators. Children who either identify as LGBTQ or are members of a family in which adult members identify as LGBTQ routinely face discrimination and ill treatment from both children and adults in schools. Because they may practice a certain religion or dress in culturally traditional clothing, children who are "other than" receive the message to "go back to your own country." Mosques and synagogues are routinely vandalized and children face the risk of violence simply for visiting their family's houses of worship.

In school settings throughout the country, students are being denied equitable access to education because they are "other than." They are the children who live on the fringes of society; the undocumented, Black, Brown, and Indigenous; the non-Christian and LGBTQ; and the disabled. As microcosms of society, schools have a long history of non-inclusive practices that prevent students from gaining access to education, and also, quite frankly, prevent the larger body of students from experiencing the benefit of a full, robust, and diverse classroom community.

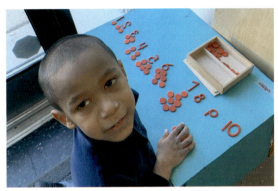

Naiim is a typically developing, highly active 5 year-old who enjoys life to the fullest. He is fully engaged in the Montessori 1 - 10 counter activity, developing concentration, independence, order and a deepening understanding of quantity and symbol association. He likes being in an inclusive Montessori classroom and being around children with varying abilities. (City Garden Montessori School, St. Louis, MO)

Black and Brown students disproportionately receive more behavior referrals, suspensions, and expulsions across grade levels than their White counterparts. Students from undocumented families fear their parents may be arrested and deported while they are at school (Fritz and Velarde, 2019), Muslim students are bullied by teachers and fellow students (Ochieng, 2017), the experiences of LGBTQ in school almost always consist of mistreatment by adults and children alike (Simon and Santos, 2018), and children with disabilities are routinely mistreated in school and excluded from the education they deserve.

Montessori education offers a method to liberate children. The preparation of the Montessori guide and the preparation of the Montessori environment can work hand in hand to create a space to accommodate diversity, and also accommodate every child's unique way of learning. A well-prepared Montessori environment can work for students from many different backgrounds (Debs, 2018) with all types of capabilities.

In the roughly 500 public Montessori schools in the United States, students come as they are and have the right to a full education with as many supports necessary to ensure their success. Many school districts and charter schools implement Response to Intervention (RtI), Multi-Tiered Systems of

Support (MTSS), and culturally responsive instructional strategies in order to meet the needs of individual learners who struggle to access the benefits of the Montessori educational program.

Both private and public Montessori schools appeal to parents who struggled in school themselves, and many families choose Montessori because they want a "better" or safer school for their children, free from the trauma they experienced as students.

As Montessori educators, we walk through our classrooms every day and see groups of children with varying abilities, all learning in unique ways. We utilize the Montessori triangle—the teacher, the student, and the environment—to create spaces and help all children reach their human potential. In Montessori classrooms, specially trained teachers and specialized materials support children's learning in a variety of ways. And multi-age grouping offers opportunities for students who learn differently to have multiple connections to learning and success, and also provides a chance for students to extend their learning above the typical content for their age. For as many ways that children are unique, there are an equal number of ways a guide can enable them to access learning.

While Montessori teacher education programs provide training in content areas such as Mathematics, Language, and Cultural studies, many do not provide the adult learners with sufficient knowledge or instructional strategies to meet the needs of children with disabilities. An essential tenet of Montessori education is self-preparation. Transformation is necessary to effectively serve children, and it is an ongoing, intentional process that enables Montessori guides to meet the specific and unique needs of students.

In this book, Ann Epstein, along with her colleague Natalie Danner, has curated and compiled an anthology of stories and support methods for children with disabilities in Montessori schools. These children are equally deserving of equitable access to education, but require additional support in their schools.

The educators who contributed to this work have raised the standard of accommodation for children in inclusive Montessori schools. They are grateful to pass on their acquired knowledge and wisdom to you, our reader.

Amira Mogaji
Vice President
American Montessori Society Board of Directors
January 2020

PREFACE

This book began as a question. "How do Montessori schools and Montessori teachers include children with disabilities?" I tapped into this question during the research and writing for my dissertation (Danner, 2015). But the question was first formed during my years as a Montessori teacher, where I guided children with and without disabilities in inclusive classrooms. I wondered why inclusion was not given more emphasis during Montessori training or at Montessori conferences. I looked for information to support my teaching and found an out-of-print book (Orem, 1969), the Circle of Inclusion research study from the 1990s (University of Kansas, 2016), and Dr. Ann Epstein's dissertation (Epstein, 1996). I eagerly read these resources but needed more to help in my day-to-day work. I sought out a master's degree program in Early Childhood Special Education. I went to school in the evenings and worked in my Montessori classroom during the day, earning my state teaching certification in special education. I felt more prepared to teach in my own classroom, but was still dismayed that Montessori teachers throughout the country didn't have similar access to inclusion training.

In order to learn more and become a researcher, teacher-educator, and advocate for inclusion, I began my PhD in Early Childhood Special Education at the University of Illinois. There, I combined my interests of Montessori and inclusion, and collected data at a high-fidelity public Montessori school for my dissertation. On my dissertation committee were three Illinois faculty members, but this group encouraged me to seek out an external faculty member with expertise in Montessori. This was a clear fit for Ann Epstein, and I'm pleased to say that she obliged.

After completing my PhD, I pitched an idea for a book on Montessori and inclusion to Ann. I was looking to create a resource for Montessori teachers and leaders who wanted more information on inclusive practices and policies. I knew there were woefully few resources available to Montessorians (Danner & Fowler, 2015). I wanted the text to represent a variety of voices: public and independent Montessori schools, teachers and school leaders, researchers and teacher-educators. And I thought that this text would be an essential one for Montessori teacher education programs to use during training, and universities to use in special education coursework to demonstrate a unique way to practice inclusion. Again, Ann generously agreed to be a part of the project.

And now, with the support of Parent Child Press, Ann's tireless efforts in coordinating and editing, and each individual author's work, this book is finally coming to fruition. We are living in an exciting time for inclusion. The American Montessori Society now offers a Montessori Inclusion Endorsement, a professional development course for Montessori teachers. Many sessions at The Montessori Event, the world's largest gathering of Montessori educators, center on how to include children with disabilities in Montessori classrooms. And webinars on inclusive practices abound.

I know both Ann and I are eager to have you read the chapters, learn from each individual story, and grow in your own inclusive practice, because each and every child, with or without disabilities, deserves full access to Montessori education.

Natalie Danner, PhD
Plambeck Endowed Chair of Montessori Education
Associate Professor of Teacher Education
University of Nebraska—Kearney
January 2020

INTRODUCTION

Children come into our lives with amazing joy, energy, and love. The Montessori approach to guiding children is rich in both curricular materials and philosophical underpinnings. This combination holds strong potential to nurture children who can soar on their own as well as children who need support.

Montessori Inclusion: Strategies and Stories of Support for Learners with Exceptionalities provides contributions from experienced Montessori special educators, teacher mentors and trainers, school heads, and organization directors. It offers both specific recommendations for assisting children and families day-to-day, as well as broader perspectives on how to effectively include learners who have a wide array of strengths and challenges in 21st-century Montessori classrooms. Montessori teachers, school leaders, policy experts, and teachers-in-training will benefit from the practical information and inspiration within.

Through vignettes that describe how teachers support children with behavioral and/or learning challenges, *Montessori Inclusion* offers readers a front-row seat to the world of children who learn and develop differently. Chapters are grouped into three areas: recommendations for blending and embracing **Montessori and Special Education**, **Current Procedures and Supports** for assisting children, and examples of **Fully Inclusive Schools**.

Montessori and Special Education

In Chapter 1, Brian Berger and Dena AuCoin combine their special education and Montessori expertise to provide a detailed, insightful synthesis of a wide range of essential inclusion components. They compare pros and cons of contracting with special education service providers as consultants versus hiring full-time special educators. They review key issues including student self-determination, staff training, program development and implementation, and collaboration. Readers are introduced to Parker, a third grader diagnosed with autism spectrum disorder. Parker's progress assists readers in learning how to successfully implement inclusion in a Montessori school. Berger and AuCoin indeed explain how Montessori and special education are "better together."

Navigating the world of special education can be daunting for experienced teachers, and truly mystifying for Montessori guides who have just completed their training. In Chapter 2, special educator and Montessorian Andrée Rolfe describes four essential components of the intersection between Montessori and special education: implications of high incidence disabilities in Montessori environments, tensions between Montessori education and special education, current best practices for special education in Montessori environments, and the importance of pursuing new information and practices to stay current in special education. A graphic that represents the intersection of special education and Montessori is particularly insightful and will be a great aid to readers.

Current Procedures and Supports

In Chapter 3, Jacqueline Cossentino and Elizabeth Slade take readers through a detailed explanation of a child study process that is rooted in Montessori principles and particularly effective in charter school settings. The authors describe their chapter as follows:

> A growing array of early intervention models aimed toward addressing diverse learning needs and developmental challenges prior to special education identification are gaining prominence in educational policy and practice. Such models are grounded in principles central to Montessori pedagogy, including mixed-age grouping, differentiation, and ongoing child study. In addition to honoring Montessori's legacy of personalized, inclusive education, early intervention models offer promising approaches to building both institutional and individual instructional capacity, enabling Montessori educators to more effectively follow not just the theoretical child, but all children.

In Chapter 4, Montessori special educator and consultant Christine Lowry shares her insightful vision for multi-tiered systems of support. She addresses current approaches to organizing levels of support in Montessori prepared environments. Her thoughtful attention to nurturing independence is particularly reassuring for guides struggling to apply interventions. Lowry encourages guides and administrators to "prevent rather than react" by preparing, managing, and guiding learners with exceptionalities.

In Chapter 5, Paul Epstein and Diane Betzolt offer a similar set of procedures well suited for independent schools. They describe practices, procedures, and documents used by classroom guides for learners enrolled at Rochester Montessori School (Rochester, MN). These include:

- observing and documenting initial concerns
- presenting documented concerns to the school's child study team
- meeting and partnering with parents
- defining learning and/or behavioral objectives and strategies
- implementing those strategies
- monitoring the learner's responses
- designing further objectives as needed.

Epstein and Betzolt build on components of Response to Intervention (RtI), designed to provide teachers with strategies to support children struggling with reading, writing, and math, as well as inattention. RtI has evolved into a broader array of supports termed Multi-Tiered Systems of Support (MTSS). Their chapter also describes several professional development meetings, and offers information on how private school administrators can help students benefit from public school resources.

What is the best way to inform a family that their child is struggling? In Chapter 6, Montessorian and special educator Cathie Perolman synthesizes over 30 years of supporting children with special needs into a heartfelt journey centering on one family. She narrates the story of her concerns, hopes, doubts, and successes as she observes the child and develops a trusting relationship with the family. She shares each step in the process, including often emotional details. Supporting children with special strengths and needs can keep us up at night. Perolman offers specific recommendations for meeting these challenges.

In Chapter 7, Ann Epstein suggests that teachers need to "make peace" with each child's present level of performance, rather than seeing academic and behavioral difficulties as insurmountable problems. Discovering "what works" can then become a positive, even exciting process. Epstein offers an array of Montessori-friendly supports for children with learning and behavioral challenges. She describes how social stories, memory guides, writing strategies, self-regulation procedures, sensory diets, and additional supports can be implemented with authenticity for children from Early Childhood through Lower Elementary levels.

In Chapters 8 and 9, Maria Eva Chaffin, Brynn Rangel, and Colleen Wilkinson, experts in the area of trauma-informed teaching, provide an overview of this critical component of effective supports. They describe adverse childhood experiences (ACEs), the effect of trauma on the young brain, and recommendations for trauma-informed teaching that align with the Montessori philosophy of learning. Sadly, if teachers are not informed, they may resort to ineffective (or worse, harsh) discipline when working with children who have experienced trauma and ACEs. Wilkinson shares her personal journey of therapeutic parenting, which offers particular insight into the deep struggles of children who have experienced significant traumas. As more schools and teachers learn to care appropriately for children who have been affected by trauma, the enormous impact on learning abilities and development can be effectively addressed.

Fully Inclusive Schools

The final chapters address two fully inclusive Montessori schools. In Chapter 10, Barbara Thompson and Pamela Shanks describe the birth of Raintree Montessori in Lawrence, KS, in the mid-1980s. And in Chapter 11, Gail Williamsen, Mandy Fuhriman, and Lizzie Dalton share the founding and evolution of Elizabeth Academy in Salt Lake City, Utah.

Thompson and Shanks chronicle the groundbreaking story of how a small school opened its doors to children with severe and profound disabilities nearly 30 years ago. They describe six implementation strategies that hold significant relevance today for any inclusive school. With profound love and appreciation for children with severe disabilities, they provide a rich array of scenarios that illustrate how and why inclusion at Raintree was successful.

Williamsen, Fuhriman, and Dalton introduce readers to Elizabeth Academy, an inclusive Montessori school that currently serves over 250 children, from infancy to adolescence. Perseverance and heart were crucial to establishing the program. Today, at Elizabeth Academy, Montessori-trained guides, special educators, and therapists collaborate to provide learning experiences that are grounded in respect and appropriate responsibilities for every learner.

These final two chapters illustrate both the promise and the reality of true inclusion. The authors offer concrete tools as well as inspiration to create and strengthen inclusion programs in Montessori settings.

Successful inclusion does not come easily, but not only is the journey worth the inevitable struggles, it is essential. No longer an aspiration, inclusion is now celebrated in Montessori schools across the U.S. Our hope is that this book offers insight and assurance for Montessorians and families who open their hearts and classrooms to children who learn differently. The authors share the joy, energy, and love that occurs when we work together to support all children. Montessori and inclusion are natural partners, and as Montessorians we have an awesome opportunity to truly follow all children, no matter their abilities.

    Ann Epstein, Primary Editor
    November 2019

CHAPTER 1

Better Together: Montessori & Special Education

Brian J. Berger and Dena J. AuCoin

Brian Berger holds a doctorate in special education and is an instructional designer for Purdue University, an adjunct professor for multiple universities, and a former special education classroom teacher of elementary and high school students. Brian's view of Montessori inclusion is as follows: "Any successful action of inclusion first begins with the ability for adults to consider the positive outcomes of that act of inclusion. Start with the positive when analyzing if inclusion is appropriate."

Dena AuCoin holds a doctorate in curriculum and teaching and administers an undergraduate program in early childhood education at Purdue University Global. She is an adjunct professor (special education and early childhood education) at Park University and Grand Canyon University. Dena is involved in research surrounding collaboration in special education and the Montessori classroom, and Response to Intervention in early childhood and in Montessori education. Dena's work has led her to a great respect and appreciation of Montessori education and the supports it can provide students with disabilities. Her intent is to broaden understanding of special education and how it enhances the practice of Montessori educators.

Parker was a third-grade boy diagnosed with autism spectrum disorder (ASD). He attended public school with an Individualized Education Program (IEP). Since entering school in kindergarten, Parker had trouble making eye contact with others. He had difficulty communicating his meaning and tended to monopolize conversations. When other children tried to talk about their interests, Parker showed evident disdain, talking only about himself. Also, he did not play much with other children at school. When his peers did not listen or when teachers made requests, he would often react with extreme behaviors. For daily support, he required a one-on-one aide.

In the middle of third grade, Parker switched to a public Montessori school. He'd been to two different schools since kindergarten and had a very difficult time; his parents were frustrated and exhausted. Someone mentioned Montessori to them as an option. Parker had no previous experience in

Montessori education, but because this was a public school, he was allowed to begin in March, in the middle of the school year. His transition to Montessori was troubling. A typical school day included Parker having behavioral meltdowns severe enough that the classroom had to be evacuated an average of three times a day. (Not every child with a disability or autism will exhibit behavior this severe or challenging.) His autism manifested in him yelling, throwing furniture, threatening others, and eventually running from the school and endangering his safety. Parker's Montessori teacher had no direct training in special education, so felt unprepared to support him. The school also had no special education service provider to help. The school staff was afraid and concerned for Parker's well-being, that of the other students, as well as the overall safety of the school.

"Montessori, Meet Special Education"

Montessori education offers families a child-centered alternative to the outcome-based model presently dictated by the public school environment (NCMPS, 2018). This educational method can attract parents of students with disabilities, as in Parker's case, especially when they feel their children are struggling in a traditional setting. Alternative school choice is fairly new in traditional education; therefore, providing special education programs has received more and more attention (Danner & Fowler, 2015; Dubovoy, 2018; Morse, 2010; Taylor, 2018).

Special Education: An Increased Presence

As the interest in Montessori education grows, an increasing number of students with disabilities may enter into the public Montessori setting (see Table 1 for the prevalence of various types of disabilities) (Cossentino, 2010; McKenzie & Zascavage, 2012). Montessori teachers will encounter the additional responsibilities for students with disabilities, which include state and federal mandates for services, and the possibility of work with conventionally trained special education providers. The Montessori value of individualization has historically claimed influence on the growth of special education pedagogy, and many Montessori professionals have success with the Montessori method alone (Leigh-Doyle et al., 2008; McKenzie & Zascavage, 2012; Vas, 2008). However, understanding of specific disabilities and the vastness of needs often goes beyond typical pedagogy (Danner & Fowler, 2015; Cossentino, 2010).

The growth of inclusion programs in schools calls for general classroom teachers to provide specific instruction. Many teachers state they feel unprepared due to a lack of skills and expertise, and report they struggle to include students with disabilities in the life of the classroom (Morton & McMenanmin, 2011). In the pages that follow, we will present information to assist Montessori professionals in exploring what kind of special education program may benefit their school, their teachers, and, most importantly, their students.

Table 1.
Student Prevalence of Disability Type in Public Schools

Disability Name	Students Identified Nationwide	Percentage of All Students
All Disabilities	7,000,000	14.0

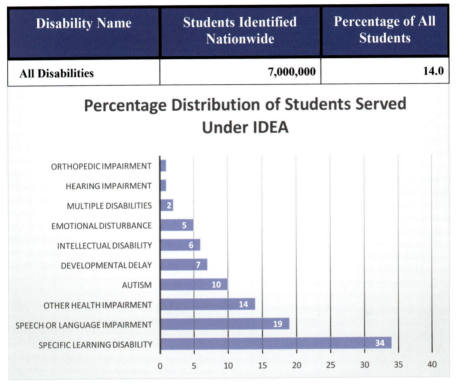

National Center for Education Statistics, 2019

Why is This Important?

Students with disabilities may need special education services for academics, as well as social and emotional issues. Disabilities impact academic, social, and emotional growth, causing deficits in areas that, when overlooked, can have lasting impact on these students. One example is the skill of self-determination: the knowledge that allows a student to understand their strengths and limitations as it relates to their personal potential (Karvonen, Test, Wood, Browder, & Algozzine, 2004). When compared to non-disabled students, disabled students showed a lack of self-determination skills (Bouck, 2004). For example, one of Parker's strengths was his ability to retain information pertaining to bird species; one major limitation was his ability to effectively communicate with peers and adults. Here, a pedagogy focus on self-determination skills would attempt to help Parker focus on both his strengths and limitations to increase his personal potential.

Since Parker lacked self-discipline, he struggled to normalize in the Montessori classroom when allowed to work freely. Due to his disability, he had difficulty communicating and having appropriate social interactions, which prevented typical normalization. A way to address this would be to teach self-determination skills such as self-awareness, choice making, and problem solving. More specifically, teaching healthy social interactions where Parker is able to share his interest in birds (his strength) and then learn to reciprocate by listening to other's interests (his limitation). Learning to consider both his strengths and limitations will increase Parker's ability to find harmony as he advances in school.

Even when exposed to the same curriculum and instruction, students with disabilities do not acquire self-determination skills as well as their non-disabled peers. Ultimately, this can lead to students not accurately recognizing their strengths and limitations in relationship to their personal interests. This can carry over into adulthood and have lifelong implications.

The Individuals with Disabilities Education Improvement Act (IDEIA, 2004; idea.ed.gov) requires that students with disabilities obtain their education in the least restrictive environment (LRE) within the public school system. The least restrictive environment often becomes the general education classroom, and the outcome is that more students with disabilities are spending the school day in this setting—hence the term *inclusion* (See Figure 1) (Eccleston, 2010; Grskovic & Trzcinka, 2011).

Figure 1.

Least Restrictive Environment	**Inclusion**
Students with disabilities should be provided education in the general education setting with their non-disabled peers to the maximum extent possible and appropriate (Alquraini, 2013; Obiakor, Harris, Mutua, & Rotatori, 2012).	A practice where all students within a school regardless of abilities or disabilities are part of the school community with access to partake in school activities together with students without disabilities, and attend their local school (Loiacono & Allen, 2008).

Meeting the needs of students with disabilities requires recognition of both their short-term and long-term needs, and an understanding of how differing disabilities impact different areas of student growth. Montessori teachers play an important role as a student's primary educator, and because an expertise in disability understanding is needed, special education professionals can add a layer of support for those students with disabilities. As Maria Montessori showed the world, students with disabilities can learn, and collaboration between Montessori and special education teachers for those students is a proposed practice (Montessori, 1912). Collaboration—direct interaction between at least two teachers voluntarily engaged in shared decision-making as they work toward a common goal—has been a common focus of research in education (Arthaud, Aram, Breck, Doelling, & Bushrow, 2007; Lingo, Barton-Arwood, & Jolivette, 2011; Musanti & Pence, 2010).

Research indicates that students with disabilities can benefit from teachers' collaborative efforts; outcomes include diminished negative behaviors, enhanced social skills, and better self-esteem (Griffin, Kilgore, Winn, & Otis-Wilborn, 2008; Nichols & Sheffield, 2014). Collaborative practices bring shared insight into student needs, can provide teachers with valuable information on how to set and meet goals in the classroom, and increase professional knowledge and job satisfaction (Arthaud et al., 2007; Cahill & Mitra, 2008; Gillies, 2014; Malone & Gallagher, 2010). Due to the rising numbers of students with disabilities in Montessori programs, both Montessori and special education teachers have an important role to play for students with disabilities and the critical practice of collaboration. This is important because often in general education, teachers can sometimes think non-disabled students are "their" students, while students with disabilities are the special education teacher's students. Collaboration in Montessori schools can ensure that each teacher feels supported in believing all students are their students. Collaboration can also encourage the expansion of Montessori practice to understand the benefit of additional support for students with disabilities.

Special Education Programming

Literature from the late 1990s and early 2000s has a focus on how Montessori materials can support students with disabilities, but little research appears to exist on the work of special education programs within Montessori schools. While contemporary research is still relatively scarce, the authors have had multiple opportunities at national conferences to share what is known about special education as it relates to Montessori. It is clear that Montessori teachers are seeking information for the changing needs of their students and wish to have the support of their colleagues.

Presently, both private and public Montessori programs have implemented various special education program approaches. For example, some Montessori programs utilize special education consultants to aid with program development, teacher-training, and limited services. Other Montessori schools employ full-time, non-Montessori trained special education teachers to maintain all aspects of special education programming (Leelanau Montessori administration and office, 2018).

A Tale of Two Programs

School administration will need to determine the level of participation the special education professional will have within a given Montessori school. We will now look at two different models: a special education consultation model and a model that uses a full-time or part-time special education teacher. The categories below incorporate many, though potentially not all, areas of consideration when developing a special education program.

Special Education Consultant Model

School A uses a consultant model. Beth, a special education expert, is hired for a finite period of time to support the school's ongoing development of special education programming. As a consultant, School A will contract with Beth and will not consider her a full-time or part-time employee. Beth is tasked with analyzing current needs and anticipating future needs for staff training, program implementation, services, collaboration, and compliancy. Beth will spend time observing the staff and school to determine strengths and challenges that can direct staff training needs and services. She will then report her findings to administration with suggestions for collaboration and compliancy. She will work with administration on overarching needs by laying out a plan for programming. Once Beth's contract is complete, the school can rehire her on an as-needed basis.

Full Time/Part Time Special Education Teacher Model

School B uses a part-time or full-time model, depending on its need. When employed part-time, Jack, a state-certified special education teacher, works 20 hours a week for School B. His overall work consists of reviewing and analyzing Individualized Education Programs (IEPs) for students, monitoring IEP goals, working directly with students on IEPs, holding meetings, and assessing student progress and needs. Jack's day at school consists of observing children who may need a special education evaluation, meeting with teachers to help them support the children with disabilities in their classroom, and attending meetings for children at School B. In addition, Jack is given time to support staff through professional development in the school year and remains available by phone and email when not at School B. Jack is not required to attend meetings outside of his weekly hours and does not have any additional responsibilities at school B, such as recess, lunch, or family nights.

When Jack is employed full-time, he works 40 hours a week. As a full-time employee, Jack conducts the same work as mentioned above and may have more students. Additionally, Jack is required to attend meetings outside of his weekly hours and will hold additional responsibilities at school B, such as recess, lunch, and family nights.

Occasional vs. Constant Presence

The fundamental difference between the consultant and full-time program is the level of presence the special education professional will have within the Montessori school (see Figure 2, page 9). Another difference in determining a program model is whether a Montessori school receives funding. (State guidelines vary too greatly to provide examples here.) Public schools are required to follow certain state and federal guidelines. For public Montessori schools, the part-time and/or full-time model may be the only option for providing special education services.

Staff Training. The first category suggests the need for special education staff-administered training. Training may be needed for a multitude of reasons, which may increase or decrease over time. Training can incorporate broad topics that address school-wide needs to support students with disabilities or more specific training that addresses single-classroom environments. A consultant will provide trainings on topics with frequency as requested or contracted by the school, based on information provided by administration and through consultant observation. Part-time and full-time employees can analyze situations and recognize needs in real-time as new challenges present themselves.

Special Education Program Development. The type of disabilities existing within a given school defines programming needs. See Table 1, page 3, for a reminder of various disabilities and their prevalence for children enrolled and served under the Individuals with Disabilities Education Improvement Act (IDEIA, 2004). Given these many possibilities, programming needs can change; however, a few disabilities overwhelmingly dominate, such as Specific Learning Disability or Speech and Language Impairment. A consultant will assess immediate needs for program development based on observation and administrative requests, and the school then implements the plan. Part-time and full-time employees develop programming to match immediate student needs and make alterations as needed, working with administration and teachers to assess on a continual basis.

Special Education Program Implementation. Day-to-day implementation of a special education program requires policy and procedures to be developed, supported, observed, and measured. Policy will communicate the programming goals intended with the program, while procedures will ensure it takes place. Constant analysis of the success and areas of need is required to continually improve the programming. A consultant will develop an initial implementation plan that leaves room for potential future changes. Part-time and full-time employees will develop programming and actively participate in implementation and maintenance of the programming plan.

Individualized Special Education Services. Students with disabilities may need curriculum accommodations, modifications, medical support, social and/or emotional supports, or may have other disability-related needs. Special education program implementation requires consideration of these and other elements. When an IEP is finalized, it is considered to be a legally binding document. All services outlined within an IEP are mandatory, not optional, as federal law considers these services as required. This includes the types of services, their frequency, and the fact that implementation of services is measurable. A consultant will provide training and suggest research-based special education approach supports and services. Part-time and full-time employees will actively adapt current programming to meet the individual daily needs of students.

Collaboration. Collaboration is a process that involves all parties, including teachers, administrators, and families, acting as willing participants working toward a shared goal. Collaboration practices may include information sharing, problem solving, and clarifying teacher strategies. A consultant will suggest collaborative guidelines and help establish initial collaborative expectations. Part-time and full-time employees will actively seek collaborative development, and can lead collaborative teams.

Federal and State Special Education Laws. State interpretation of federal law demands that a special education professional be aware of changes, state focuses, and localized trends. Programming needs will also be influenced by state mandates as they are interpreted from federal laws. States will often make changes to support proven need-areas with special education populations. A consultant will understand (and help a school understand) relevant special education legal concerns. Part-time and full-time employees will understand and share relevant laws, and they can adapt practices due to state and federal changes to special education laws.

Private Information Compliancy. The Family Educational Rights and Privacy Act (FERPA) protects the privacy of education records for all students; however, there are further considerations for students with disabilities (FERPA, https://www2.ed.gov/policy/gen/guid/fpco/ferpa/index.html). These considerations span grade reporting, maintaining special education files, disability confidentiality among some staff, and many other considerations. A consultant will suggest a plan for file compliancy. Part-time and full-time employees will actively maintain and monitor special education compliance.

In Figure 2 below, some of the broader considerations for involving a consultant versus a part-time or full-time special education professional are highlighted. If a school answers 'yes' to the question prompts, a consultant may be appropriate, and if the answers are 'no,' a part-time or full-time professional is likely needed.

Figure 2. **Special Education Programming Considerations**

Special Education Programming	Considerations: Consultant vs. Part-Time/Full-Time
Staff Training	Will the school know when or what training is needed?
Special Education Program Development	Will the school maintain appropriate special education programming and know when to alter/request further consultation?
Special Education Program Implementation	Will the school as currently staffed be able to implement the plan?
Individualized Special Education Services	Will current teachers implement appropriate special education programming independently after training? How will that be ensured and/or encouraged?
Collaboration	Will the school conceptualize, promote, and maintain needed collaborative practices?
Federal and State Special Education Laws	Can the school ensure that changes are implemented when mandated?
Private Information Compliancy	Can current school practice also support the addition of special education paperwork without part-time or full-time special education support?

Copyright © 2015 (Berger)

Parker's Journey

The administration at the Montessori public school understood they needed to help Parker and other children with disabilities. They hired Anna as a full-time special education teacher for the upcoming school year. Anna reviewed Parker's file and history, met with teachers and administrators, and met with Parker and his family at the start of his fourth grade year. Anna began the school year in September by collaborating with Parker's teacher and educating her on noticing his triggers as well as signs that he was struggling with social and emotional needs. Anna, Parker, and the teacher met and discussed his likes and dislikes in the classroom; together, they made a list of things he liked that he could choose when he needed to calm down. These choices were used to help him from running from the classroom or expressing himself with extreme anger. Initially, Parker was given as many breaks as he felt he needed, with visual supports in picture form for making choices and learning to make alternative choices when necessary. Parker was provided with a one-on-one aide and a complete visual schedule with pictures. In the beginning, he was assigned a designated space in the classroom to complete his work. Initially, a schedule was created each morning and afternoon through collaboration between Anna and Parker's Montessori teacher. By October, Parker and his aide would complete his schedule each day. By the end of November, Parker was participating in creating his own schedule. At that point, Anna introduced a "to do" list where Parker would write out his schedule for the day. In December, Parker was completing his "to do" list independently and participating in the morning work cycle. This demonstrated the development of self-determined behaviors with appropriate choice-making skills. By the end of January, Parker began to use his own daily planner and incorporate at least three choices of work in each Montessori work cycle.

In November, Anna and the IEP team created a behavior plan for Parker to help develop his skills in following teacher requests, following his daily schedule, and being with peers. Since he had been working closely with Anna, his teacher, and his aide since September, he was successful about 70% to 80% of the time, and by April he was highly successful, as evidenced by Figure 3. In addition to collaboration, scheduling, and behavior interventions, the IEP team developed a matrix that mapped Parker's day and the various academic and behavioral interventions he needed to find success. After monthly assessment and work, the team was able to help Parker find harmony and normalization in the Montessori environment and effectively reduce his resource and aide support from 5½ hours a day to about 30 minutes.

Figure 3. **Parker Behavior Intervention Plan Data**

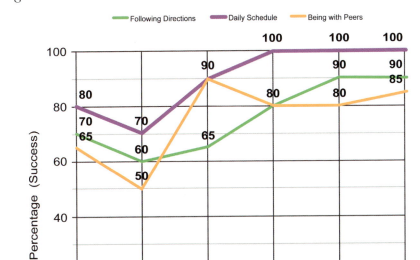

Figure 4. **Parker: Matrix of Needs and Supports**
*Universal support = typical classroom support

Work Cycle • Math • Science • Social Studies • Language Arts	Needs support and reminders during academics.	For support: • Assigned work space • Keyboarding • White board • Work Cycle checklist with increasing independent choices • Preferred/non-preferred activity offering • Choice board for preferred activity • Visual reminders	**Universal Support**
Class Meeting	Needs reminders and encouragement to remain engaged.	• Choice board • Visual cues • Calming activities • Visual cues +/or social stories • First/then visual support	**Universal Support**
Lunch	Working toward more appropriate behaviors during lunch. He requires monitoring and guidance for peer interaction.	• Choice board	**Universal Support**

What to Do?

As Table 1 (page 3) demonstrates, many millions of special education students are currently identified within public schools. Successfully adding special education programming is possible for any public Montessori school. Administrators will need to weigh the differences based on current and projected needs, financial realities, and school growth. Consultants can help provide support, as needed, for schools with more static enrollment and low special education numbers. Full-time professionals can help quickly growing schools, those with high special education numbers, and schools with high variance of disability types. Many schools may choose to begin with a consultant and move toward full-time as the program grows and develops. Choosing to employ a special education consultant or a part- or full-time special education professional can lead to a supportive and inclusive program.

Montessori and Special Education

As Montessori educators, the first curriculum is to *follow the child*. What does this mean when it comes to special education? The authors' research to further illustrate the connection between Montessori and special education led to a realization that both Montessori and special education teachers strive to advocate for the same thing. Implementing a special education program in a Montessori school should be considered an expansion of practice, not a surrender of philosophy.

Revisiting the Beginning

Dr. Maria Montessori originated her work with children from a psychiatric hospital who were labeled as insane, mentally ill, and emotionally troubled. As an effect of Montessori's work, those children began to learn new skills and increase their level of accomplishment (Adcock, 1990; Donabella & Rule, 2008). Furthermore, Montessori's own studies began with Jean Marc Gaspard Itard and Édouard Séguin, both believed to be innovators in the discipline of special education as evidenced by their work with Victor, "The Wild Boy of Aveyron" (Gitter, 1967). (See Chapter 2 for more information about Itard and Séguin.)

Montessori teachers have been called cousins of special educators; the Montessori method includes individualized teaching and learning rate (Cossentino, 2009; McKenzie & Zascavage, 2012). The clear history of the Montessori method and special education has shown the need to investigate contemporary Montessori schools to determine how to support students with disabilities and how to guide schools to efficiently meet student needs (Epstein, 1994).

Parker's Continued Success

Since the successful implementation of special education services, Parker has continued to grow and find normalization within the Montessori setting. Following are notes from his most recent observation:

- Parker gets out a rug and unrolls it. He paces around the room one time and then sits down next to the rug. He is setting up the blue word cards on the rug. He has them all lined up on the rug. He gets up and gets his writing notebook from the academic file bin where he is supposed to put his work. He brings the notebook to the floor and he gets his pencil. He begins to write in his notebook. It appears as though he is writing the words in some organized manner. Parker finishes his work, and though he needs reminding to pick up his rug and put it away, he follows through.
- A student comes over and hands Parker his yellow notebook. Parker gets up and walks over to the student and says, "Hey, why did you bring this notebook to me, it belongs in the basket?" The student explains that the teacher left it on her table. He walks over to teacher (with his hand on his hip) and says, "Um, Sally, this notebook belongs in the basket." She tells him something and he walks back to his work table and sets the notebook on his table. He sits back down and continues to work.

Montessori schools are watching the growing number of students with disabilities choose the Montessori method of education (Cossentino, 2010). In the experiences of the authors, the similarity of the two disciplines has led both Montessori and special education teachers to desire working together in almost every situation explored. Better together: Montessori with special education.

"Alone we can do so little; together we can do so much."
—Helen Keller (Shaker, 2014)

CHAPTER 2

What New (and Not So New) Montessori Teachers Need to Know About Special Education

Andrée Rolfe

Andrée Rolfe, EdD, spent 35 years working in public special education as a teacher, learning consultant, and administrator before becoming AMI Elementary-certified in 2013. Currently, she is an educational consultant for AMS and AMI schools. Andrée believes strongly that Montessori education can serve almost all children in a way that is developmentally healthy. She works to support guides as they expand their capacity to work with more children who present with learning challenges.

Every new Montessori guide is familiar with the story of Dr. Maria Montessori's early work with profoundly disabled children from the asylums of Rome and how the methods of two special education pioneers, Dr. Jean Marc Itard and Dr. Edouard Séguin, influenced the development of Montessori pedagogy (Kramer, 1988; Montessori, 1909/1967). Like Itard, Maria Montessori recognized the role of the environment and critical periods for learning. Like Séguin, she believed that intellectual deficits were an educational problem and that children would benefit from an individualized approach, beginning with training the senses and developing practical skills of everyday life. Maria Montessori extended Séguin's work and created her own methods for writing and reading. Her success with children who were considered to be uneducable drew international attention. In 1900, she shared what she learned as a special educator in the Montessori Lectures on Special Education (Montessori, 1969). As the story continues, she then applied that knowledge to the education of typical children in the first Casa dei Bambini (Children's House) in the San Lorenzo tenements of Rome, starting a movement that continues to resonate all over the world today.

Over a century later, special education and Montessori education still share essential elements: a focus on the individual child, sequential experiences with concrete materials, and teachers who are trained to observe and make decisions based on those observations. Montessori schools have often been viewed as a good fit for children who present with specific challenges because of the hands-on learning, teachers who are committed to following the child's development, the inherent flexibility of multi-age classes, and the inclusive nature of Montessori communities (Engelfried, 2018; McKenzie & Zascavage, 2012; Pickering, 2017; Pickering, 2019). Some parents of children with identified special needs opt for a Montessori program when their child starts to attend school. Other parents seek out a Montessori education after a child has encountered difficulty in a traditional setting, anticipating that the benefits of a Montessori program will enable their child to thrive. Today's Montessori schools report that they are serving children with a wide range of special education diagnoses (Kahn, 2009b) as well as many children with undiagnosed learning needs. In fact, it is suggested that more than 15% of the children in Montessori schools present with special education needs (Cossentino, 2010).

The similarities between Montessori education and special education provide the potential for success in serving all children in Montessori environments. While Montessori education and special education are clearly compatible, there are real and significant differences between the two models. These differences give rise to specific tensions that are experienced as challenging, frustrating, and sometimes insurmountable to new Montessori teachers. This chapter will focus on what new Montessori teachers need to know about special education, the differences between Montessori education and special education, and how those differences can be bridged through more inclusive Montessori training. While the content is vital for those who are starting out, it is also valuable for experienced teachers, especially those who may have children with varied needs in their classrooms.

Montessori Training in the 21st Century

The century-old tradition of Montessori teacher preparation is unique among teacher preparation programs. Montessori training offers theory linked to practice, an expectation that trainees will master technique as a craft (as opposed to an art or a science), and a coherent vision in which teaching truly aligns with children's learning (Cossentino, 2009). Across the major Montessori training programs (American Montessori Society (AMS), Association Montessori Internationale (AMI), International Montessori Council (IMC), and Montessori Educational Programs International (MEPI)), the course of study focuses on the oral transmission of Dr. Montessori's developmental theory and extended practice using the materials she designed to aid the development of the senses and the intellect. There is a strong emphasis on observation as a skill that is learned and a habit that is established through many hours spent intently observing children in Montessori classrooms (Montessori, 1917/2007). A transformation of the spirit is anticipated as the adult learner absorbs and integrates Dr. Montessori's vision of the teacher as a guide whose role is to support the child's self-construction of her personality, social self, intellect, and morality (McFarland, 1993; Montessori, 1949/1995).

Montessori theory does not suggest a unique approach for children with learning and behavioral challenges. The developmental stages are considered to be universal, with differences in development arising from obstacles the child encounters. The Montessori mandate is to "follow the child" by observing the child's needs, removing obstacles in the prepared environment, and then connecting the child to that environment. The teacher is to interfere as little as possible with the process of self-construction (Montessori, 1949/1995). New Montessori teachers enter their classrooms anticipating that they will be the person who will meet the exceptional needs of their students and that they will do so within the context of Montessori practice.

Special Education in the 21st Century

In the last quarter of the 20th century, Congress passed a series of landmark laws ensuring the rights of individuals with disabilities. The Individuals with Disabilities Education Act (IDEA, 2004) guarantees children with disabilities (ages 3 through 21) a free and appropriate education in the least restrictive environment, most often considered to be the child's local public school. Today, 13.7% of all children enrolled in today's public schools are identified with disabilities and are receiving special education services (NCES, 2018).

Once a child is diagnosed with a disability that adversely affects her educational performance, she is determined to be eligible for special education and related services. The child's education is guided by an individualized education program (IEP) with a timetable of measurable goals and objectives (Smith, Tyler, & Skow, 2018).

Special education training has evolved dramatically over the past century. The specialized knowledge and skills to be mastered were set forth in The Council for Exceptional Children's (CEC) Initial Level Special Educator Preparation Standards (2012). The Council for the Accreditation of Educator Preparation (CAEP) requires that these standards guide special education courses and teacher preparation programs in colleges and universities (CEC, n.d.). Key elements include: understanding how development and individual learning differences interact; creating safe, inclusive, and culturally responsive learning environments; mastering general and specific curricular content knowledge; using assessment and data to inform educational decisions; adapting evidence-based instructional strategies; adapting ethical practices and becoming active professionals; and developing collaboration skills and practices. New special education teachers enter classrooms ready to take direct action in remediating identified areas of weakness and supporting children as they participate in general education settings.

Special Education in Montessori Schools

Newly trained Montessori teachers accept positions in private, charter, and public schools. Private Montessori schools, with limited access to public funds for some special education and related services as mandated in IDEA 2004, need to develop their own models of support for children with special needs if they are to be able to accept and serve children with learning and behavioral challenges. More traditional private programs adhere strictly to Montessori guidelines and offer informal supports provided by the classroom teacher. Many private schools integrate suggestions made by outside specialists, and others employ a tutor model implemented by Montessori teachers with additional special education training (Kahn, 2009a). Private Montessori schools often work with local school districts to access the add-on services that are available to children who are identified with a disability. Another model involves collaboration with a local university to provide a range of special education supports implemented in a Montessori style (Shanks, 2009). More recently, some private Montessori schools have developed school-based intervention systems of tiered Montessori-based supports (Cossentino, 2010).

In contrast, the more than 500 public Montessori programs (National Center for Montessori in the Public Sector Staff, 2019) *must* provide a full range of special education and related services, according to IDEA 2004. Typically, special education and related service personnel, who are not Montessori trained, are provided to these schools by the local school district. Guidelines for charter Montessori schools vary, with many hiring special education teachers and related service providers using public funds.

Fresh from training, many new Montessori teachers find themselves unprepared for the special education challenges they face. Regardless of program level or school type, they will most likely encounter situations requiring knowledge of special education terminology, awareness of disability-related challenges, familiarity with special education interventions and accommodations, and collaboration with related service providers such as speech therapists, occupational therapists, and behaviorists. New Montessori teachers working in public schools must work within Montessori guidelines *and* be compliant with local, state, and federal special education requirements (Murray & Peyton, 2008). They face the additional challenges of integrating push-in and pull-out services throughout the day, becoming informed about special education practices outside of the Montessori curriculum, preparing children for high-stakes testing, and, sometimes, co-teaching with special educators who are not Montessori trained. As they grapple with the responsibility of serving two sets of job expectations, they may soon conclude that Montessori education and special education are more different than alike.

Special Education Training for Montessori Teachers

The Montessori community has acknowledged the need for additional training in special education, and comprehensive training is available for experienced teachers in the field. MACAR (Montessori Applied to Children At-Risk) training is offered through Shelton School in Texas. In 2015, AMI started a two-summer Inclusive Education course in San Diego. In 2018, AMS launched a Montessori Inclusion Endorsement that involves a combination of on-site instruction, online courses, and field work (G. Lofquist, personal communication, October 2019). The Endorsement is currently offered through two programs: West Side Montessori School Teacher Education Program in New York, NY and Shelton Teacher Training in Dallas, TX. Some Montessori teachers pursue state certification and take special education courses at local universities. Public and charter schools provide professional development in special education during the school year.

For Montessori teachers-in-training, some training programs offer a master's level program consisting of traditional Montessori training plus university coursework at an affiliated university, including a special education course. One such program is offered by AMI training centers in affiliation with The Center for Montessori Education at Loyola University (Maryland). Newly certified teachers can complete three graduate courses at Loyola University to earn a Master of Education degree in Montessori Education. In 2015, the author redesigned Loyola's Introduction to Special Education course to address the needs of the new Montessori teacher. Adult learners explore disability categories, supports, and practices and then focus on this question: *What will this special education knowledge mean for me in my Montessori classroom?* They become aware of the differences between special education and Montessori education and consider the steps to take to bridge those differences in their Montessori classrooms.

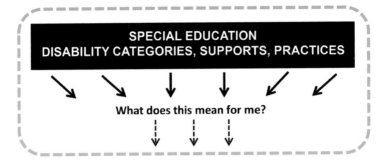

What New Montessori Teachers Need to Know

To prepare new Montessori teachers to work in their classrooms with children who present with disabilities, four topics need to be explored and considered through a Montessori lens:

- The implications of high-incidence disabilities in Montessori environments
- The tensions between Montessori education and special education
- The value of current best practices for special education in Montessori environments
- Staying current: the pursuit of new information and practices in special education.

Descriptions of these topics are provided below. Suggestions for exploration activities are offered in the sidebars. Learning resources (books, videos, and websites) are included in the Suggested Resources list (References, page 164).

Exploring the Implications of High-Incidence Disabilities in Montessori Environments

High-incidence disabilities are those that are most prevalent among school-aged children (Smith et al., 2018). These disabilities account for 96% of the children served through IDEA 2004 (NCES, 2018): learning disabilities (34%), speech/language impairments (20%), other health impairment, including attention deficit hyperactivity disorder (ADHD) (14%), autism

> **ACTIVITY FOR EXPLORATION**
>
> In The Stuttering Foundation's video, *Straight Talk for Teachers*, school-aged children speak openly about the disability and how they are affected. Viewing followed by discussion leaves a lasting impression. New Montessori teachers can consider how to integrate specific accommodations in the classroom.

spectrum disorder (ASD) (10%), intellectual disabilities (6%), developmental delays (7%), and emotional disturbance (5%). It is likely that new Montessori teachers will encounter children with these high-incidence disabilities in their first job assignment. In order to be successful guides for these children, teachers first need to acquire a working knowledge of the causes, characteristics, and challenges presented by each of the high-incidence disabilities. Then they need to consider how the characteristics might manifest across the planes of development, what disability-specific obstacles a child might encounter in a Montessori environment, and the current perspectives about each disability.

What sources can be used to explore high-incidence disabilities? Special education texts provide basic information about each of the disability categories. Online learning resources, such as the IRIS Center at Vanderbilt University (iris.peabody.vanderbilt.edu) offer interactive web-based instructional modules. Fact sheets are posted on numerous disability-related websites. Short videos are powerful tools that convey what a disability is like for a child and enable new Montessori teachers to extrapolate the variables that they will need to examine. See the Suggested Resources list (References, page 164) for video links.

> ACTIVITY FOR EXPLORATION
>
> Articles by leaders in the field should be read and their ideas should be debated. Taking on the distinct viewpoints of Dr. Russell Barkley, Dr. Thomas Armstrong, entrepreneurs with ADHD, and Dr. John Ratey in a simulated debate prepares new Montessori teachers to enter into discussions about ADHD within their school communities.[1]

Within each disability category, there are contrasting voices to be heard and understood. New Montessori teachers need to become familiar with the multiple perspectives that guide current thinking about ADHD, ASD, and auditory processing disorders.

Exploring the Tensions between Montessori Education and Special Education

Montessori education and special education differ with regard to their foundational models and the imperatives behind inclusion, vocabulary, delivery of support, and assessment of growth. Once these differences are recognized and understood, new Montessori teachers can begin to consider what they can do to bridge those differences and resolve the following tensions they will encounter in the field:

Tension #1: Montessori model versus special education model. Maria Montessori formulated a developmental model of human growth from birth to age 24, which serves as the theoretical north star of Montessori education. The model incorporates four distinct phases during which the evolving infant/child/adolescent/young adult presents with qualitatively different sets of psychological, intellectual, and social characteristics as well as different sets of needs during the long and natural process of self-construction (Montessori, 1971). Development occurs when universal, innate human tendencies (orientation, order, exploration, abstraction, imagination, work, repetition, precision, control of error leading to perfection, the mathematical mind, and communication) interact with an environment that invites the expression of those tendencies (Montessori, M. M., 1956). The Montessori vision for education is concerned with how to assist the child to develop her potentialities in ways that are self-directed and guided by innate tendencies, personal interests, and the characteristics of the child's developmental plane.

The special education model evolved out of the medical model of diagnosis followed by treatment using a problem-solving approach (Smith et al., 2018). Special education combines specially designed instruction, support, and services for children with an identified disability to meet the unique educational needs of a child. The purpose of special education is to enable students to develop to their fullest potential and be career-ready or college-ready by the end of their high school years.

It is critical that new Montessori teachers understand that Montessori education is based on a developmental model of self-construction, while special education is based on a medical model in which specific interventions and accommodations give rise to remediation and adaptation. The models are inherently different, providing the backdrop for the tensions that arise in practice.

> **ACTIVITY FOR EXPLORATION**
>
> Consider successful mixtures of Montessori and special education models in public and private schools (Jones & Cossentino, 2017 and NAMTA Journals: Spring, 2008, Spring, 2009, Summer, 2014). Analyze the compromises made to mix the models.

The Building Bridges chart (next page) illustrates the differences between Montessori education and special education with regard to the models, guiding principles for inclusion, the language used, delivery of instruction, and assessment. An educational mixture, with each model retaining its essential properties, is the ideal resolution. The middle column in the chart that follows describes the work that leads to the resolution of these tensions and the development of an inclusive environment that is capable of supporting all learners.

BUILDING BRIDGES

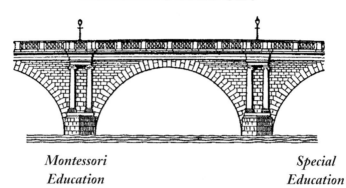

Montessori Education   *Special Education*

	Montessori Education		Special Education
Model	Developmental Self-Construction Whole-Child Child time: In her own way, in her own time	**Resolution Found In:** Belief that both models support the development of children with learning differences	Medical Diagnosis--> Intervention Problem-Specific Age/Grade-based expectations
Inclusion	Everyone is included and contributes to a community Preparation for life A human imperative	**Resolution Found In:** An inclusive community that complies with required special education regulations	Compliance with federal/state regulations Free & appropriate public education in the least restrictive environment (FAPE in LRE) A legal imperative
Language	Montessori terms Deviations, obstacles	**Resolution Found In:** Everyday language	Special education terms Eligible for services based on diagnosed disability
Delivery	Exploration/choice Indirect preparation Waves of interest/cycles of work Change environment Teacher as sole guide	**Each Model Needs to Honor:** Choice/autonomy/independence Practice to mastery	Direct instruction Continuum of service delivery Goal-driven Change child Collaboration with other providers
Assessment	Rigorous observation Child's work	**Each Model Needs to Consider:** How do you know what the child knows? Use of data	Demonstrated mastery of specific objectives at timed intervals

Tension #2: Inclusion in Montessori education versus inclusion in special education. Belief in inclusion is woven deep into the fabric of Montessori thought and is an imperative borne out of being human. In Montessori, education is a preparation for life, a life in a society in which everyone participates and makes their own unique contribution. For some Montessorians, the charge is reframed to preventing exclusion, rather than promoting inclusion (Goertz, 2001).

In the special education model, including a child in the least restrictive environment is a legal imperative. Parent advocates and disability advocates demanding their civil rights, were joined by legislators in the second half of the 20th century (Smith et al., 2018). The culminating legislation, IDEA 2004, guarantees every child with a disability the right to an individualized education in a school environment that is as close to typical as possible. Inclusion is mandated through compliance with federal and state regulations. Procedural safeguards are in place to protect the rights of parents and their child and to give families and schools formal mechanisms for resolving their disputes (IDEA, 2004).

> **ACTIVITY FOR EXPLORATION**
>
> Examine websites of Montessori schools (private, charter, and public) and discuss what can be inferred about each school's inclusion model from the mission statements, admissions policies, and supports for children with special needs.

Tension #3: Language in Montessori education versus special education. Montessori educators and special educators use vocabulary that can be experienced as two different educational languages. Each model has its own nomenclature to describe children, their needs, and how those needs are addressed. For new Montessori teachers, having an acquaintance with terms such as *language impairment* or *accommodations* and acronyms such as *LRE (least restrictive environment)* does not ensure a deeper understanding of what the terms translate to in practice. This results in confusion and misunderstanding as new Montessori teachers read evaluations and attempt to decode the meaning of the individualized plans that are developed for children with disabilities. The language differences also present a formidable obstacle when working with special education professionals and parents.

> **ACTIVITY FOR EXPLORATION**
>
> AuCoin & Berger's vocabulary matching activity (2015, tinyurl.com/y4j4r3hb) results in lively conversation about the differences in seemingly compatible terminology. New teachers can depict the degree to which paired Montessori and special education terms are alike/different (e.g., grace and courtesy/social skills training using Venn diagrams.

A common language base is a necessary prerequisite to productive communication. New Montessori teachers first need to become familiar with special education terminology and then consider what that terminology means from a Montessori perspective. A common vocabulary needs to be established in order to bridge the gap and prevent meaning from "sailing past each other darkly" (Goertz, 2001, p. 72), when Montessori teachers and special educators talk. New Montessori teachers should master the nomenclature of special education. They need to know the IDEA disability categories and be able to name and describe common special education acronyms (e.g., FAPE, LRE, IDEA '04, IEP, IFSP, RTI, PBIS).

Tension #4: Delivery of Montessori education versus special education. In a Montessori classroom, the teacher links the child to the environment, presenting developmentally appropriate materials and activities to the right child at the right time. Children have the freedom to choose their activities and older children determine how they will organize their time. Deep concentration and independence are valued as children satisfy their waves of interest. Learning is thought to proceed indirectly as well as directly. If a child is not progressing, the teacher looks to change an aspect of the environment or offer more lessons to the child in the area of concern.

Special education is most often delivered through direct instruction. Lessons are goal-driven and designed to remediate deficits in the context of general education standards. The child engages in teacher/specialist-directed practice until mastery is achieved. The learning environment is determined by the child's needs and the IEP team's decisions, ranging from separate schools, to pull-out and push-in services, to collaborative teaching in general education classrooms.

Most Montessori educators and special educators think very differently about delivery. Montessori teachers wonder why special education teachers need to take children away from their chosen work and impose lessons and practice regardless of the child's motivation to do so. They often do not see the value of focusing so intently on a child's weaknesses. Special educators and related service providers do not understand the Montessori curriculum and wonder how children learn in classrooms where teachers do not teach in traditional ways. Their mission is to deliver a service and produce measurable results. Student choice and freedom with responsibility can seem inappropriate from the special education perspective.

The first step in resolving this tension is examining one's belief system about collaboration. The central question to consider is: *Do I believe that what I will do with others for this child is better than what I can do alone?* New Montessori teachers need to know that if their answer is no, then attempts to collaborate with others on behalf of a child will fail. The ability to serve all the children requires constructive collaboration, which is a complex process.

Collaboration between and among educators in Montessori schools is best conceptualized as a **style** for direct (but not directive) interaction between **co-equal partners** who are **voluntarily involved** in **shared decision-making** as they work toward **common goals** on behalf of a child (Friend & Cook, 2007). This working definition can be used as a starting point for honoring the Montessori principles of choice, autonomy, and independence and the special education principle of practice until mastery is achieved.

Tension #5: Assessment in Montessori education versus special education. In Montessori classrooms, detailed observation of the child is the key to assessing a child's strengths and needs, with an emphasis on being objective and non-judgmental (Montessori, 1918/2007). New Montessori teachers are aware of the paths a child may take to move through developmental sequences. They observe, reflect, and make changes in the environment in response to the emerging needs of the child. Progress is evaluated on a daily basis: during lessons, when looking at a child's independent work, when reviewing a work journal, and/or in conferences with students (Lillard, 2017). Children evaluate their work with direct feedback from the materials. Progress evaluation is indirect and noted informally in the teacher's records. If an obstacle is noted that the teacher is not equipped to address, a typical response would be to seek out someone who is specially trained in that area for advice.

For the special education teacher, assessment is a direct, frequent, and systematic means to document progress in meeting predetermined goals. At timed intervals, the teacher collects data and makes a judgment as to whether the child has met a goal or not. Then, a next goal is formulated, based on the child's area of deficit and the long-term objectives for that child's development as set forth by the IEP team.

These questions are central to the topic of assessment: *How do you know what the child knows? What can the child do independently? What can the child do with support?* The systematic collection and use of data run counter to the indirect and holistic Montessori approach. In special education, growth is quantifiable and data drives instructional decisions. To resolve this tension, new Montessori teachers need to understand how data is used in special education, how instructional goals are developed, and how skill growth is assessed. They need to think about how they might adapt their progress monitoring techniques in order to document progress towards IEP goals. A child at the Primary level (ages 3–6) who has a language delay might have this IEP goal: *In response to the teacher's morning greeting, the child will produce intelligible 3- to-4 word utterances without additional prompting on 4 out of 5 mornings.* With guidance from the speech-language therapist, the Montessori teacher would systematically record the child's exact responses in order to analyze the utterances and document growth. This data would then inform the child's next language goal. Dr. Steven Hughes (2009), Allison Jones & Jacqueline Cossentino (2017), and Dr. Joyce Pickering (2019) all speak directly to Montessori beliefs and offer strong arguments for the value of evaluations by specialists and assessing progress through more direct use of data.

Exploring the Value of Current Best Practices in Special Education

Special education offers a multitude of best practices across disability categories. Some are easy for new Montessori teachers to envision. The following practices are easily incorporated into a Montessori vision: Peer-assisted learning for children with learning disabilities, sensory diets for children with sensory needs, social stories for children with autism spectrum disorder, functional curricula for young children with intellectual disabilities, and accommodations for children with diabetes. In contrast, discrete trial training within the Applied Behavioral Analysis approach for children with autism, functional behavioral assessments and interventions for challenging behaviors, an FM system (a wireless system that transmits sounds directly from a teacher's microphone to a child's receiver) for children with auditory processing disorders, data-based practice for self-regulation of attention, and assistive technology using iPads are often not seen as compatible with a new Montessori teacher's thoughts about the prepared environment.

> **ACTIVITY FOR EXPLORATION**
>
> Construct a knowledge base about a special education topic (e.g., sensory processing, anxiety disorders, selective mutism). Identify the challenges that children encounter, strategies and interventions suggested, and the accommodations indicated for a child in a specific plane of development. Sources: internet sites (associations, institutes/schools), video presentations by leaders in the field, and articles by Montessori writers.

New Montessori teachers need to become comfortable considering what might be necessary for a child with a disability to be included in their classroom and how they can embrace a special education practice and "make it Montessori." Critical to this way of thinking is familiarity with what is currently working in the greater Montessori community. New teachers can expand their vision after learning about a Montessori approach to autism (Lane, 2009) or reading an

AMI trainer's reasons for using the Orton-Gillingham sequence with children who have dyslexia (Awes, 2012). They can increase their ability to connect children with the environment by becoming familiar with supplemental materials for buttoning (Shanks, 2014) and an occupational therapist's recommended adaptations for children with sensory processing disorder (SPD) (Noddings, 2017a, 2017b, 2017c). Awareness of how Montessorians incorporate best practices in special education can facilitate the understanding that some children need supports outside of Montessori practice until they are ready to engage in specific aspects of traditional Montessori education.

Staying Current: The Pursuit of New Information and Practices in Special Education

Special education practices reflect current thinking about disabilities and current state and federal rules and regulations. Unlike Montessori practice, change is frequent and inevitable in special education. Montessori teachers need to stay up-to-date and know where to go for information when a child receives a new diagnosis, an unfamiliar support is proposed, or state requirements change. They need to think through the dynamics of partnering with families and consider the important information that parents provide regarding the impact of a child's disability. Inclusive Montessori training should provide time to explore disability websites and examine various state forms including IEPs, Individual Family Service Plans (IFSP), 504 Plans, and sample Response to Intervention (RtI) or Multi-tiered Systems of Support (MTSS) plans. Information is plentiful, so it is important for new teachers to enter the field with a set of familiar and reliable internet resources.

> **ACTIVITY FOR EXPLORATION**
>
> With a simulation of a parent request (e.g., *My child has been diagnosed with PANDAS and will need accommodations*) or a new IEP provision such as assistive technology for dysgraphia, new Montessori teachers locate credible information to inform their approach and develop responses to parents or a plan for IEP compliance.

More Inclusive Training in Special Education for New Montessori Teachers

What do new Montessori teachers need to know about special education? They need to understand the implications of high-incidence disabilities, recognize the reasons for the tensions that exist between Montessori education and special education, realize the value of current best practices in special education, and know how to access reliable information on short notice.

How can new Montessori teachers acquire this additional expertise? Possibilities include special education seminars during training or webinars soon after training ends, a graduate level special education course/module taught or co-taught by someone who is Montessori trained, and professional development in-service work within the first year of teaching. While the time available in a graduate course is ideal, the topics and activities presented in this chapter can be easily adapted for other delivery options. Special education knowledge is important to the success of new Montessori teachers. More inclusive Montessori training will prepare new teachers for the reality of the special education challenges they will face in the field.

---

1. Dr. Russell Barkley is a clinical psychologist who is recognized as an authority on attention-deficit hyperactivity disorder (ADHD) in children and adults. He believes that ADHD is a developmental disorder that is biologically based (Barkley, n.d.). Dr. Barkley's research offers strong support for the use of stimulant medications in the multi-modal treatment of ADHD.
Dr. Thomas Armstrong is a psychologist and an educator who writes extensively about learning and human development. He believes that attention-deficit disorder is a not a valid medical diagnosis, but rather a set of context-dependent behaviors that exist as a response to the complexities of modern times (Armstrong, n.d.). Dr. Armstrong recommends an array of holistic strategies (including diet, neurofeedback, cognitive and psychosocial strategies, and physical activity) to support the child's development.
Successful, young entrepreneurs celebrate the characteristics of ADHD that provide them with an advantage in their work: creativity; multitasking; risk taking; high energy; and the ability to hyperfocus (Archer, 2014, May 14). Insight and adjustments have enabled them to maximize their strengths as entrepreneurs.
Dr. John Ratey is a clinical psychiatrist who is known as an authority on the brain-fitness connection. He believes that ADHD is a biological brain disorder and advocates that exercise should be included in the treatment regimen because it can reduce or eliminate the need for medication (Medscape, 2009, Oct. 08).

CHAPTER 3

Following All the Children: A Montessori Model of Tiered Instruction

Jacqueline Cossentino and Elizabeth G. Slade

Jacqueline Cossentino, MEd, EdD (1964–2019), began her Montessori career as a parent, and quickly extended to researcher and administrator, as well as university professor. An ethnographer by training, Jackie drew from her direct experience as head of an independent Montessori school and principal of a large urban public Montessori school to produce an internationally recognized body of scholarship on Montessori education. At the time of her death, she was a lecturer in Loyola Maryland's Montessori Studies program. She regarded child-centered, asset-based approaches to serving children with special needs as a central ethical mandate of Montessori education. Jackie said, "Too many children are labeled, isolated, and served in ways that impede rather than release their potential. And too many of those children are black, brown, and low-income. Activating the best of Montessori education so that all of us can follow all of the children is an urgent need."

Elizabeth Slade, MFA, has been a Montessori educator since 1987, with roles including teacher, mentor, coach, coordinator of teaching and learning, and school leader. She was the founding coach at the National Center for Montessori in the Public Sector, and has worked to support the growth of the method in public schools across the country. She is AMS- and AMI-credentialed (Administrator and Elementary, respectively). Her daughter, Bella, has inspired her to think in a broader way about what schools are capable of offering to support all children. Extensive work in public Montessori schools has only confirmed Elizabeth's understanding that this method, built on observation, is a way to reach all learners, and has fueled her deep faith in the ability of people to shift their minds in order to make space for everyone to thrive.

American educators—including Montessorians—are witnessing significant increases in the number of students with learning difficulties in their classrooms. In recent years, both researchers and practitioners have noted a rise in attentional issues, autism spectrum disorders, and sensory integration difficulties. Possible factors are increasing amounts of time with screens, environmental toxins, aging parents, or more systematic identification (McFarland, J., Hussar, B., Zhang, J., Wang, X., Wang, K., Hein, S., Diliberti, M., Forrest Cataldi, E., Bullock Mann, F., and Barmer, A., 2019). And the rise in incidence crosses ethnic, racial, and economic lines (though children in poverty continue to be more likely than their more affluent peers to be identified for special education services) (Schifter, L.A., Grindal, T., Schwartz, G., & Hehir, T., 2019). Children with diverse learning needs constitute a growing segment of the nation's classrooms, and they are changing the face of schooling.

Most public schools report a special education population of between 11 and 15 percent (Snyder, 2016). While reliable figures on similar populations in independent Montessori schools are more difficult to track, anecdotal reports suggest that the incidence may be closer to 22% (Snyder, 2016; Pickering, 2003). Regarded by many as congenial to learning differences, parents often seek Montessori (and other independent) schools when their children demonstrate difficulty in "regular" school. That such students are served in Montessori schools, many without benefit of formally mandated individualized education plans (or the bureaucratic procedures that accompany them), would seem to lend credence to the idea that Maria Montessori was, herself, a special educator and her method constitutes the world's first inclusion model of support services.

To be sure, it's difficult to argue the historical resonance of this claim. Montessori launched her career working with special needs students after having studied the work of French psychologist Édouard Séguin, one of the patriarchs of special education. Likewise, her emphasis on hands-on, differentiated, self-paced learning guided by intensive and ongoing child study provides a template for best practice in both general and exceptional classrooms (Gresham, 2002; Lillard, 2005). Moreover, that Montessori environments provide opportunities for free movement, choice, and extended periods of deep concentration helps explain what appears to be a lower-than-average incidence of attention-related difficulties, as these pillars of Montessori pedagogy also happen to be treatment strategies for ADHD (Pickering, 2003; Rief, 2008). Perhaps most important, Montessori educators are trained to regard every child as exceptional and, in response, to hold flexible, individualized instruction in the highest regard (Cossentino, 2009, 2017; Lillard, 2017; Montessori, 1949/1988).

In a foundational way, Montessorians are, at the very least, close cousins of special educators. In the course of daily practice, however, theoretical and dispositional affinity can only go so far. When learning differences become learning disabilities, even the most sensitive and resourceful of teachers can be pushed beyond the limits of their expertise. Too often, the frustration that comes with an inadequate skill set prompts teachers and schools to conclude that the child with special needs does not "fit" in a regular school environment. "We don't want to set the child up for failure" or "We don't have the resources to adequately serve your child" are explanations offered to the parent whose child has been screened out of an independent school. In public schools, where such screening is illegal and where the stakes for poor academic performance are high, the situation is different. As educators in the public sector confront the challenge of guiding all students toward academic success, the policies and practices associated with prevention, early screening, and identification of learning needs have moved to the center of the enterprise of schooling. This chapter is about the lessons that accompany that challenge, and their particular applicability to Montessori educators.

In fact, the trajectories of Montessori and special education, particularly early intervention, intersect in important ways. Historically, Montessori theory and practice have influenced the development of special education pedagogy. In some cases, as in Ireland, Montessori training and special education training have been explicitly combined. In other cases, Montessori practices such as child study, the use of manipulative materials, and a focus on choice and individualization have made their way into special education pedagogy through subtle cross-fertilization among practitioners. More recently, however, developments in special education policy have begun to influence Montessori practice.

What follows is an examination of why and how that influence has evolved as it has. More important is to probe the potential of recent developments in special education policy to enhance Montessori practice. What are the natural affinities between special education and Montessori practice? What specific pedagogical moves lie at the core of following the child? How might Montessorians more effectively leverage the unique properties of the prepared environment and the prepared adult to better serve all children? The answers to these questions illuminate how progressive, data-informed approaches to identifying and responding to students with learning differences can make the process of following the child more transparent, more equitable, and more successful.

The Case of Serena

Consider the following case, a composite drawn from several Primary/Early Childhood (3- to 6-year-old) classrooms in public Montessori schools.[2] Serena is a 3-year-old girl, in her first year at the school. While she was born in the U.S., English is not her first language, and Spanish is the main language spoken at home. Upon entering the school, Serena spoke little English or Spanish. She was unable to maintain focus on any activity for more than a few minutes, and then only with the assistance of an adult. When not supervised closely, she tended to crawl on the floor, hide under tables, and disturb other students as they worked. After observing this behavior, and despite all her attempts to engage Serena for the first two weeks of school, Serena's teacher, Helen, concluded that both she and Serena needed help.

By mid-September, Serena was on the agenda of the Primary instructional team's weekly meeting.[3] The team, comprised of fellow Primary teachers, the school social worker, English as a Second Language (ESL) teacher, and the assistant principal, followed a protocol designed to structure discussion so that it would lead to the development of an Action Plan for Serena. After presenting her case, the team was invited to ask clarifying questions about Serena. The team learned that the only work Serena currently stayed with for any length of time was the Pink Tower[4], that she often wore princess clothes, and that she had a cat named Arlene. Following these clarifying questions, the team contemplated how best to articulate Serena's key challenge. With the understanding that there were likely many challenges confronting Serena, the team nevertheless needed to choose one to form the basis of the Action Plan.

Based on the clarifying questions and the additional discussion they stimulated, the team zeroed in on the challenge of choosing work. The hundreds of options available in the Montessori 3–6 environment were likely overwhelming for Serena. Learning to operate within this environment would mean being able to both choose work and concentrate on it for more than a few minutes.

---

2 Cases quite similar to Serena's exist in a variety of schools. Public schools, however, are more likely to feature the full spectrum of support services, and constructing the case around such a program allows description and analysis of an ideal case.

3 Prior to attending the meeting, Helen met with Serena's parents. Family engagement in this process is key, though not described in detail here.

4 The Pink Tower is an iconic Montessori material. It has 10 pink cubes of different sizes, from 1 centimeter up to 10 centimeters, increasing in increments of 1 centimeter. The material, which is part of the sequence of sensorial work, is designed to provide the child with a concept of "big" and "small." The child starts with the largest cube and puts the second-largest cube on top of it, continuing until the smallest cube is placed on top.

Clarifying the challenge then led to articulating a goal for Serena—one that could be observed, measured, and evaluated within the next four to six weeks. Helen identified the goal of independently choosing and completing one piece of work each morning. With the goal identified, the next step was to come up with strategies the teacher might employ to meet the goals. For this she turned to her colleagues.

For the next 5 minutes, the room was silent as each team member wrote as many ideas as possible that could be incorporated into a Montessori work period. When the time was up, upwards of 30 ideas had been recorded on sticky notes, which were displayed in clusters for Helen to survey and assess. Suggestions ranged from "limit her choices to two or three" to "have her work with an older student" to "introduce new Sensorial materials."

From the bank of strategies, Helen chose two. Based on one team member's insight that Serena likes the color pink (Pink Tower, princess pink, and Arlene is the pink cat from the cartoon Garfield), the first strategy was to create a series of Practical Life activities that used pink items—soap, scrub brushes, fabric, cloths, and so on. Helen commented that she noticed that when Serena did the Pink Tower, she was very precise and the thought that perhaps she would enjoy activities that capitalized on precision, such as using tongs. Another teacher (who had a daughter who also loved pink) offered to loan her the pink tongs she had at home and assist with the setup.

The second strategy centered on Serena's cat, Arlene. The ESL teacher had a series of simple animal matching cards that she thought Serena might like. This prompted another teacher to remember that he also had some animal cards featuring sizes of pets with a number of cats in the set. And this prompted Helen to recall that she had a series of cat books at home that she could bring in for Serena. "Creating high-interest work around cats" was added to the Action Plan with the ESL teacher and the other teacher listed as support. The social worker thought these animal cards might be an easy way for her to talk with Serena about her habit of crawling around and hiding under tables as being more cat-like and to help her begin to move in the classroom in a more appropriate manner. This, too, was added to the Action Plan as a weekly date between Serena and the social worker.

Figure 1. **Excerpt from Serena's Action Plan**

Today's Date	Action What will be done with/for student or group? e.g., intervention, service, instruction	Responsible Person Name and Position	Timeline		Progress Monitoring Evidence the action was successful or not
			Start Date	Monitor Dates	
9/29	Create new Practical Life work using pink tools and items. More Practical Life!	Helen & Jeanette	10/5	11/10	Work log/frequency chart tracks work completion and length of concentration
9/29	Use ELL animal naming cards as a hook to work Also, Frank's pet cards and cat picture books	Helen & Julia & Frank	10/1	11/10	Work log/frequency chart tracks work completion and length of concentration
9/29	Weekly time in class with Social Worker (30 minutes)	Maria	10/5	11/10	

Progress Monitoring: (Did the student meet the objective?)
Please date the appropriate response(s):
_____Objective met, continue interventions
_____Objective met, increase objective to _____
_____Some progress, continue intervention and monitor
_____No progress or deterioration, refer to TIER Two

As the discussion of strategy selection concluded, Helen collected all 30 suggestions and placed them in an envelope, so that she could use the others as needed without waiting for another meeting. Helen agreed to evaluate the success of the chosen strategies through daily documentation of work choices and concentration spans. The team set a progress-check for 6 weeks hence. If the goal had been met, the team would set a new goal. If not, they would consider more intensive support. Helen left the meeting with 30 new strategies, a commitment to implementing three of them, and renewed interest in exploring what would work for Serena. The conversation had piqued her curiosity about Serena's interests, her likes and dislikes, and what made her tick. Helen was now ready to partner with Serena to guide her in finding her place in the classroom community rather than simply trying to get her to behave in a less disruptive manner.

Six weeks after this initial session, Helen reported on Serena's progress. Using a simple frequency chart, Helen tracked both the amount of work Serena was able to complete for each of the 30 days of the strategy, and the length of time she was able to sustain concentration during a given work period. After 6 weeks, the progress was uneven, but the data revealed a trend: Serena was able to meet her goal 75% of the time. She thoroughly took to the pink Practical Life activities and now was even engaging in messy water work so long as she could use a pink bucket or sponge. The new cat work had revealed a general interest in animals and Serena was now increasing her vocabulary through her use of the Farm.[5]

Throughout the year, Serena remained on the team's radar. Her action plan was updated two more times, and records of progress were shared with her family and maintained in Serena's cumulative file. By the time she arrived at her second year, Serena had developed strategies for interacting appropriately with peers and had increased her concentration spans significantly. She no longer hid beneath tables. She chose work from all areas of the room—though she continued to prefer Sensorial and Practical Life to Language and Math—and she greeted adults with a smile and a cheerful "hello" each morning.

Child Study: What's Going on with This Child?

The process described above constituted the first step in a three-layer process known variously as early intervention, Response to Intervention© (RTI), and Multi-tiered Systems of Support (MTSS) (Cummings, et al., 2008; Miller, B., Taylor, K., & Ryder, R. E. , 2019; Tilly, 2008). At this school, it was known as Child Study. We recommend the use of this somewhat old-fashioned term because it references what we suggest is the core work of the process: to understand the child. Unlike many similar processes practiced at schools across the country, the foundational question posed by this team was not, "What's wrong with Serena?" or "What interventions should we offer Serena?" but "What's going on with this child?"

What is perhaps most remarkable about this case is that Serena's progress was directed almost entirely by a team of Montessori Primary (3–6) teachers, and that was by design. With the exception of a weekly visit with the school's social worker, Serena's Action Plan was entirely grounded in the work of the Montessori prepared environment—a highly structured, yet flexible learning environment designed to meet the unique needs of each child at his or her unique developmental journey. In contrast to recent reports on the failure of RtI to resolve learning challenges in an effective and timely manner (Balu et.al., 2015), the process described here was highly effective because the response was, by design, rapid, thoughtful, and grounded in ongoing observation and documentation.

Was Serena "fixed"? No. Despite her evident behavioral and attentional progress, Serena remained a child who was learning English and whose

---

5 The Farm is a miniature collection of objects representing a farm. It is used for language development, specifically the function of words, in the Montessori 3–6 program.

command of English was weaker than that of her peers. However, this process resulted neither in referral for special education services nor a complete exit from the system. Rather, it enabled a team of educators to maintain systematic and collaborative focus on Serena, how she learns, what she needs, and what obstacles may be in the way of her optimal development.

Remaining on the team's "radar" meant focusing its attention on isolating the source of Serena's language difficulties. Because her case called for additional clinical expertise and more intensive support, midway through the year she moved into the second stage of the early intervention process. Following a preliminary consultation with the school's speech-language pathologist (SLP), the team developed new goals aimed toward helping Serena develop phonemic awareness and increase her vocabulary. Because the SLP's initial consultation indicated that in-class strategies were yielding demonstrable progress, the team, in consultation with Serena's family, concluded that the Montessori language program, which is heavy on phonics and vocabulary building, was the best match for Serena's current needs. Strategies matched to her goals included daily one-on-one practice with Sandpaper Letters, "I Spy" games, and the Mystery Bag. In addition, both Helen and her assistant made a point of inviting Serena to interact verbally with peers and recorded the nature of those interactions as part of daily recordkeeping. Finally, the team invited the SLP, who maintained a part-time case load 3 days a week at the school, to observe Serena twice before the next review of the case, which would take place 4 weeks from the completion of the new action plan.

It is likely that Serena will remain in the team's awareness throughout her years in Primary, and probably into her Elementary years. At age 4, it is still too early to determine whether Serena's language difficulties are severe enough to qualify her for special education services or accommodations. However, the team understands that early attention to difficulties in oral language can, in many cases, sufficiently resolve issues to enable the child with delays to become a proficient reader and writer, and that the most effective time for addressing language issues is prior to the age of 5. Likewise, had the challenges Serena displayed at age 3 gone unaddressed, her behavioral issues would have likely masked the obstacles affecting her language development.

That sort of "miss" is all too common, even in Montessori classrooms, where ongoing observation, documentation, and modification are, ideally, hallmarks of all instruction. The consequences of inadequate observation, attention and progress monitoring can be grave. For a child like Serena, those consequences could range significantly from reading delays to accumulated losses in other areas, and from misdiagnosed social/behavioral disorders to inappropriately targeted special education services.

The Promise and Peril of Tiered Instruction

Moreover, without a rigorous and ongoing process to consider the question of "what's going on" with children, students like Serena, who inevitably would be found deficient in behavioral as well as academic performance, would almost certainly be identified as learning disabled and placed in special education. And once such identifications were made, much of Serena's education would be in the hands of adults other than her classroom teacher. Increasingly, however, progressive, data-centered approaches to supporting students are enabling teachers and schools to interrupt that cycle and redirect children like Serena toward a path of holistic and responsive support, in which needs and instruction are carefully matched.

The idea of "match," as psychologist J.M. Hunt (1961) put it, has been central to Montessori practice from the beginning. It's also what prompted reform-minded educators and policy makers in the 1960s to advocate for significant investments in early intervention as a means of enhancing the life chances of children placed at risk. Head Start, one of the key programs to emerge from Lyndon Johnson's Great Society, was built on the premise that boosting early learning would constitute a comprehensive and consequential intervention in the lives of poor children and families. Among other benefits, Head Start was expected to boost IQ, improve parenting skills, and provide access to basic health and welfare services through community based, federally funded support (Rose, 2010).

At precisely the time that the Office of Economic Opportunity, under the direction of Sargent Shriver, was devising plans for Head Start, Montessori education was experiencing a rebirth in the United States and news of the method was spreading among psychologists like Hunt, educators, and well-to-do parents. Indeed, Shriver's in-laws, the Skakels, were instrumental in the founding of the Whitby School, one of the nation's first Montessori schools (Whitescarver & Cossentino, 2008). Other Montessorians experimented with Montessori classrooms in impoverished communities in initiatives that foreshadowed Head Start programming (Gitter, 1965). Not surprisingly, Montessori was identified as one of several models for Head Start. While not linked to official special education policy—that would come a decade later with the passage of the Education for All Handicapped Children Act of 1975 (EHA)—the rise of Head Start, with its implicit focus on early intervention, added one more connector in the chain linking Montessori and special education.

In 1990, EHA was renamed the Individuals with Disabilities Education Act (IDEA), which both identified rights for students with disabilities and mandated differentiated instruction based on individual children's needs. While the core tenant of IDEA—that all children are entitled to individualized instruction—bears a striking similarity to Montessori's mandate to "follow the child," gaps between theory and practice were pronounced from the law's inception. After nearly 3 decades of criticism prompted by advocates for children with disabilities, Congress embarked on a substantial overhaul of the act.

The most significant outcome of the 2004 reauthorization of IDEA was a provision for employing early intervention ("early intervening services") as a means of determining eligibility for special education services. In the past, students who were suspected of having significant learning disabilities were identified through a series of tests designed to measure the difference between the student's intelligence and his or her scholastic achievement. In instances where the discrepancy was significant, a student qualified for specialized instruction and related services. Criticisms of procedures associated with the discrepancy model included claims that too many students were inappropriately placed in separate settings; that they did not receive appropriate services when served in regular classrooms; that they were denied access to related services such as speech or physical therapy and psychological counseling; and that disproportionate numbers of minority students were identified (NCD, 2002).

By contrast, tiered instructional models aim to create a filter designed to both target specific learning difficulties and distinguish developmental from instructional issues. Tiered instruction locates substantial responsibility with classroom teachers, and when implemented effectively, reduces the number of students identified for special services and increases the likelihood that support will be appropriately targeted, monitored, and demonstrably effective (Cummings, et al., 2008; Fuchs & Fuchs, 2006).

As the demand for evidence of tiered instruction as a gateway to special education eligibility has risen, school systems have responded in creative ways. Tiered instructional systems now exist in 32 states, and districts continue to make substantial investments in structural, procedural, and instructional capacity in order to comply with the stipulations of IDEA. As schools mobilize around the concept of multi-tiered levels of instruction, teachers are redefining their systems for data collection, assessment, and the instructional decisions that follow. School schedules must include time for team meetings, and administrators must hone their skills as participants in, as well as leaders of, rigorous and ongoing data-informed deliberation.

While data collection and analysis are critical to the success of these systems (and great sums of money have been invested in creating and maintaining data management products), the true center of tiered instruction remains the concept of "match." Data are only useful when they help match a student's needs with appropriate assistance. And that depends entirely on the capacity of teachers to make sense of the observations, tallies, and scores they compile. Tiered instruction, in other words, calls teachers to be, in Maria Montessori's words, both "scientist and saint" (Montessori, 1949/1988).

Child Study as a School-Wide Priority: Implementing a Viable Process

Montessori schools that organize themselves around child study commit to two key goals. The first is to focus intensively on children in the first plane of development (birth to age 6). The second is to establish and follow a structured process for responding to all children's needs in a manner that is both rational and individualized. Both commitments maximize the natural strengths of Montessori pedagogy. Both commitments also push teachers to stretch their analytic and diagnostic skills and schools to build bridges between the prepared environment and the wider educational community.

A well-functioning child study process works like a funnel, with the largest number of student issues addressed through Tier 1 modifications, leading progressively through more intensive interventions toward the final step of referral for special education services.

Figure 2: **Tiered Instruction as a Funnel**

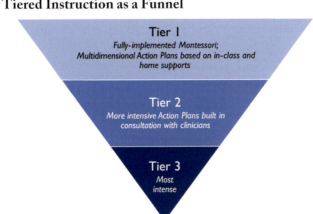

As a practical matter, child study means, most obviously, catching difficulties before they turn into insurmountable obstacles. Infant, Toddler, and Primary teachers serve as the child's first prepared adults. In order to follow every child, these adults must mobilize their skills at observation, environment design, and flexible lesson presentation so that atypical behaviors are noted early, followed meticulously, and addressed daily in an adjustable adaptive approach. In a system that functions well, first-plane teachers will have the largest and most fluid case load, and most of those cases will involve children between the ages of 3 and 5.

Accounting for the full range of developmental issues, schools can expect between 25% and 30% of their primary students to make it to the first step of the process (Tier 1). Schools with higher numbers of bilingual students or English Language Learners (ELL) can expect that percentage to rise. Issues will range from speech delays to sensory integration and autism spectrum concerns, most of which will present during the child's first months at the school, to executive function and reading difficulties, which will become more evident between the ages of 4 and 5. In all cases, the central questions for Primary children in the first tier of intervention revolve around normalization: Who is moving toward normalization and who is having difficulty? What obstacles are impeding optimal development? What modifications can be made to remove obstacles?

In addition to naturalistic observation, Tier 1 supports can be well served by basic diagnostic screening instruments. In order to gather baseline data, many schools institute screens such as the Peabody Picture Vocabulary Test to all entering students. The June Shelton School and Evaluation Center in Dallas, TX has devised a series of diagnostic tools aimed specifically for Montessori students (Pickering, 2001).

While many issues, particularly those related to speech and early reading, can be resolved during the Primary years, students who have not exited the child study system by the time they are 5 are likely to be candidates for more intensive intervention and, possibly, special education referral. In these cases, documentation of the relative success or failure of strategies employed is essential for effective intervention and/or special education placement.

Regardless of when a child enters formal child study, the process is designed to expedite problem-solving by adhering to specific procedures and time limits. For instance, a student on a Tier 1 action plan who does not demonstrate progress within a controlled time frame will move on to Tier 2. At this secondary level, clinical professionals are brought into the deliberative process as the team shifts its focus toward a more intensive diagnostic approach to intervention. Tutoring, speech therapy, counseling, and other related services may be recommended for the child at Tier 2. For schools that employ full-time or consulting clinicians, the process calls for strategic scheduling so that consultants may attend meetings, collect and share data, and generally participate in the work of the team. Schools that do not employ such professionals should, at the very least, develop relationships that allow for occasional consultation and referral.

If Tier 2 interventions are unsuccessful, the child may likely be headed toward qualifying for special education services. Tier 3 supports are the last stop before identification and, as such, they often mirror the type of services provided by special education teachers: one-on-one programmed instruction, intensive therapy, and, in some cases, accommodations similar to those the student may expect once he or she is deemed eligible for services. Progress monitoring at this stage matches the intensity of the interventions.

While the child is always the central focus of the work of early intervention, that work is made possible by collective deliberation. Known variously as "instructional teams," "program level teams," or "data teams," these groups of between four and eight professionals are the engine of the process. In order to make the most of Montessori expertise, teams should be organized by program level. Depending on the school's enrollment, team meetings should be scheduled to address one to two cases in a 60-minute session, with time for follow-up on each case within four to six weeks. Weekly meetings are optimal, and all meetings should follow a standard format, including protocols for preparation, discussion, and time-keeping.

For most teachers, including Montessorians, the deliberative process requires both practice and support. For this reason, meetings should be convened by a designated facilitator, whose role consists of maintaining case dockets, creating and announcing agendas, and ensuring that meetings proceed according to agreed-upon norms. Working well as a team takes time and trust. Once the structure and norms of the meeting are established, team meetings become a venue for serving students as well as fostering teacher development.

From Data to Knowledge to Service: The Child-Centered Community of Practice

The holistic, integrated nature of Montessori pedagogy can, for some Montessorians, feel at odds with the clinical, rationalized systems of tiered instruction and special education. Terms such as "data," "action plans," and "intervention" can be off-putting to educators who are more accustomed to talking about "sensitive periods," "language explosions," and "cosmic education." But a closer look (and listen) reveals that child study, particularly when implemented by thoughtful Montessori teachers, gets to the heart of Montessori pedagogy. Child study's emphasis on precise documentation coupled with the social, deliberative requirement of teamwork illuminate what, for many, is a mysterious and evanescent undertaking. Child study gives us a process and a language for talking about what teachers actually do when they follow the child.

Child study is, above all, a collaborative process that exemplifies the power of collective deliberation in transforming data points into usable knowledge. Teachers who engage in child study report immense satisfaction with the process for three key reasons. First, the collaborative deliberation about a particular student places the child at the center of the enterprise. Second, structured discussion about instructional strategies both values the collective expertise of the team and makes practice visible by unpacking the discrete moves that compose a teacher's pedagogy. Third, the systematic and precise chronicle of progress is more likely to produce successful results than the solitary trial and error that characterizes the professional life of many teachers.

Figure 3: **The Child-Centered Community of Practice**

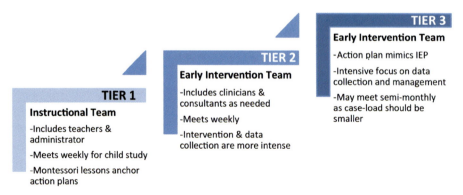

Practitioners who share common language, practice, and goals, and who work together to create and use knowledge, are known as "communities of practice" (Brown & Duguid, 1991; Wenger, 1998). Communities of practice share some similarities with "professional learning communities" (DuFour, 2004), particularly when they exist in schools. However, a key distinction revolves around the intersection of identity and practice. Where professional learning communities are working groups dedicated to the enterprise of improving teaching and learning, communities of practice exist in many settings; orchestras, athletic teams, scholars of particular disciplines, chefs, carpenters, and other artisans often belong to communities of practice. And unlike professional learning communities, which direct their energies primarily toward the achievement of outcomes, communities of practice exist to deepen the practice of their members.

The community that comprises an orchestra, for instance, devotes its collective effort to expanding, refining, and sharing musical knowledge, partly for the sake of improving the orchestra's performance and partly for the sake of deepening the musicians' shared understanding of their collective music-making. Practice, in other words, functions as the embodiment of the community's purpose. The relatively closed system of the community of practice, characterized by mutual engagement, joint enterprise, and shared repertoire, also characterizes the professional culture of Montessori educators (Cossentino, 2005, 2009).

When applied to Montessori schooling, a well-implemented early intervention process strengthens the community of practice by providing structure and transparency to the work of following the child. Grounded in principles of Montessori pedagogy, team meetings provide a venue for colleagues to develop as well as to share expertise. Because the team's practice entails the creation and management of knowledge, clinical language is part of the process. And because that practice centers on serving the child according to Montessori principles, the bulk of deliberation revolves around understanding and removing obstacles to development, refining particular Montessori presentations, or developing more sensitive approaches to providing support without impeding independence. In this way, the collective work of early intervention serves as both a manifestation and a fulfillment of Montessori pedagogy.

Put another way, if early learning, child study, and differentiation are what Montessori is all about, then Montessori is all about early intervention. Schools that make early intervention an institutional priority (shared by teachers at all levels as well as parents) can maximize the power of Montessori pedagogy—making practice visible to all members of the community and increasing the odds that all students will be served.

CHAPTER 4

An Overview of a Montessori-Based Multi-Tiered System of Support

Christine Lowry

Christine Lowry, MEd, is committed to serving students with learning and behavior needs. She has founded, directed, and taught at two inclusive Montessori schools serving students from Toddler through Elementary. Christine shares her many years of experience by offering professional development, consultation, and coaching to Montessori educators, public and private Montessori schools, districts implementing Montessori education, and at state and national Montessori conferences. She teaches Montessori/special education courses using a real-time, online format. Christine values the benefits and philosophy of the Montessori system of education for its ability to serve and support all kinds of learners in our current times. She sees Montessori classrooms as a pedagogy for offering inclusive educational programs.

The numbers of students with a variety of learning and behavior needs is on the increase. In both Montessori and conventional schools and classrooms, school leaders and classroom educators are asking for the knowledge, understanding, and skills they need to best support *all* students in their classrooms.

The trend for the past 20-plus years, driven by the field of special education in response to the Individuals with Disabilities Education Act (IDEA), has been to serve all students in the least restrictive environment (LRE). Recent figures from the National Center for Education Statistics (2019) indicate that 14% of students (3–21 years of age) have been identified for special education services (an increase from 12%). As of 2018, of this percentage, 63% (ages 6–21) were spending 80% or more of their time in general education classrooms. One might guess that in Montessori schools, 100% of students with unique needs are being served 100% of the time in their general Montessori classrooms.

We know that inclusive classrooms that guide each student on a path of meaningful learning and social-emotional growth benefit all students (Rosen, P.; Inclusive Schools Network, 2015). Some of these benefits include:

- Differentiated individualized instruction for all
- Academic supports for all
- Behavioral supports for all
- Respect for and acceptance of diversity
- Effective use of school resources

How do we as Montessori school leaders and educators create a school-wide inclusive community and still provide a high-fidelity Montessori education? A Montessori-based Multi-Tiered System of Support (MTSS) is one framework that can provide an answer.

A brief history of 20-plus years traces the evolution of providing equitable education services for our children and youth, birth to 21 years of age.

- 1997: Reauthorization of the Individuals with Disabilities Education Act (IDEA) provides free and appropriate public education (FAPE) in the least restrictive environment (LRE). This includes Positive Behavior Interventions and Supports (PBIS).
- 2001: The Pyramid Model, a framework for promoting positive emotional and social growth and specific interventions for challenging behaviors is developed and introduced.
- 2004: Response to Intervention (RtI) is introduced in the reauthorization of IDEA as an alternative model for identifying students with specific learning disabilities. The framework was then expanded to include all students with diverse needs.
- 2010: The Prevent-Teach-Reinforce Model was introduced as a standardization of the PBIS model.

In 2015, with the reauthorization of the Elementary and Secondary Education Act (No Child Left Behind), renamed Every Student Succeeds Act (ESSA), PBIS and RtI were not mentioned, but were replaced with the Multi-Tiered Systems of Support framework. MTSS is to be an "umbrella" approach that addresses student need for support with learning and social-emotional needs. ESSA allocates Title I, II, and IV funds to implement this framework at the state, district, and school level. Each state and district was expected to have an MTSS implemented in 2019.

A Multi-Tiered System of Support is based on the recognized importance of linking learning and behavior with an interdependence of classroom management and instruction. A "Prevention vs. Reaction" framework focuses on strategies to minimize challenges in behavior and learning with tiers of support from Tier One best practices, targeted supports at Tier Two, and individualized interventions at Tier Three. Ongoing formative assessment and progress monitoring provides for each student as their needs are addressed across each tier.

The three tiers are a continuum of support. All students will benefit from Tier One best practices. A student who needs a more targeted instructional and/or behavioral plan to learn a social skill or academic concept will continue to benefit from Tier One practices while receiving the additional supports of Tier Two. Once both Tier One and Tier Two practices have been fully implemented, there may still be a very small number of students (one or two in a typical classroom) whose needs are more intense and frequent and who require a Systematic Individualized Intervention Plan in addition to the Tier One and Tier Two supports already being provided.

The Montessori-based Multi-Tiered System of Support is consistent with the framework of "Prevention vs. Reaction" that stays true to our best practices within the Montessori philosophy, pedagogy, and curriculum. It is a model that is meant to be school-specific for large, small, public, charter, and independent schools, with a design that is doable, manageable, developmentally appropriate, and beneficial at all levels of Montessori education.

As Montessori school leaders and educators, we begin our task with reflection. To successfully support all students, we must look at our beliefs, our assumptions, and our biases. It has been found that teacher attitude toward inclusive classrooms is the most critical to that success (Ross-Hill, 2009; Elliott, 2008). As we commit to serving all students, we need to cultivate the beliefs that:

- All children are unique individuals with strengths and challenges
- All children want to be respected, accepted, and included for a sense of belonging
- Behaviors are communication of need
- Behavior and learning cannot be separated
- There is no single "cure," or model, for categories of special need
- A child is not a label; a diverse need is not a deficit
- Behavior can change

- Best practices benefit all children
- Inclusive classrooms benefit all children

A Montessori-Based Multi-Tiered System of Support

Tier One: Prepare

As Montessori educators, we know how to design and prepare an environment for the plane of development and level we teach. We attend to the physical, emotional, social, and learning environment in our classroom. When we create an inclusive prepared environment, we must attend to all those with the "best practice" details to support the needs of all students—including those dealing with sensory processing issues, attention issues, social and communication issues, learning issues, chronic stress/trauma issues, and the emotional issues that tend to coexist with each of these.

We begin with a physical environment that is aesthetically pleasing, has minimal visual and auditory "clutter," a room arrangement for movement and whole-group, small-group, and individual options for work space, and well-organized and sequenced curriculum areas with thoughtfully displayed materials and activities. Careful attention to the details that will support children's independent engagement with materials is needed.

We explicitly and carefully plan a classroom climate that is positive, responsive, attentive, and cultivates nurturing and responsive relationships with adults and peers. We use responsive guidance techniques that convey respect and acceptance of each student. We create a predictable daily and weekly schedule with clear and taught routines, and well-structured transitions. We teach clear, consistent expectations for behavior and learning. We intentionally engage in activities to develop a positive, socially cohesive classroom community of students. We teach social-emotional skills and embed these throughout the school day.

Our learning environment must engage every student. We use scaffolded instruction, provide opportunities for repetition, self-paced learning, and freedom of choice with responsibility. We use ongoing observation of readiness and prior knowledge to inform and impact our lesson planning and instruction so it is responsive to each student.

Creating a peaceful classroom includes Grace and Courtesy lessons, teaching social-emotional skills, and engaging each student in learning. But it is responsive relationships and guidance that is the foundation of a positive, supportive, and well-managed classroom.

Each student deserves our respect and acceptance. Cultivating a responsive and nurturing relationship with each student, based on their behavioral, learning, and cultural needs, can be a challenge. Developing an understanding of the personality, traits, strengths, and challenges of our students are our tools for building relationships, providing responsive instruction and any accommodations that might be needed. Through observation, conversation, and attending to the ways that students respond to instruction, we can begin to intentionally respond to each student's behavior as communicating a need. This is, in large part, what Tier Two strategies (see the next section) are all about.

Our children at each age and level are developing executive functioning and self-regulation skills. In fact, we now know that these continue to develop long past even young adulthood. For a peaceful classroom that benefits all students as well as educators, intentionally creating opportunities to develop in these two areas is important, especially so for those who are experiencing learning and behavior difficulties. In the Montessori classroom, we have so many "built-ins" that encourage executive functioning and self-regulation. The structured freedom that allows for choice of activity, activities that develop concentration and planning, repetition through self-paced learning, exploration, and problem solving are all integral to Montessori philosophy and pedagogy.

Our understanding of tools for development of self-regulation is deepening. Dr. Montessori understood through observation the importance of incorporating the Silence Game, Walking on the Line, limiting identical materials, teaching Grace and Courtesy, and conflict resolution. And though she did not use the term "self-regulation," this is the direct result of these activities and skills. We can add to our repertoire with a Quiet Space (a corner that is visually closed to the classroom for one child to practice breathing techniques), and other self-calming tools. We can intentionally teach, model, role-play, and practice a number of self-regulation and social-emotional skills with our students throughout the year.

Tier Two: Manage

With our relationship with each student and our observations, we will be able to identify those students who "seem to be stuck." Maybe it's a concept, a skill, an academic area, or difficulty with an executive functioning or social-emotional skill that is limiting this student's learning or interactions with peers and adults. We observe that this child needs additional supports to "get back on track." Tier Two provides targeted teaching, learning, and behavior supports as additions to our Tier One best practices.

Differentiated instruction responds to the individual's need for what to teach, where and when and how often to teach, how and how much to teach, and makes adjustments to the "traditional" lesson, or presentation, to best meet the student's needs. The instruction, the content, and any product, therefore, is adapted to the "targeted" goals for the student.

Some of our students may need accommodations in addition to the intentionally prepared components of the environment. These are the strategies, techniques, and tools that support equitable access and participation. For example, a child who needs an aid to see properly would need the accommodation of glasses to equitably participate. A child who has significant attention difficulties might need an especially prepared workspace to aid his attention needs. A child needing a high degree of structure and predictability might need a visual schedule of the day and, perhaps, a work plan. A student with anxiety and sensory needs might need access to the "heavy work" of some Practical Life activities.

A student with social and emotional difficulties might need specific lessons to teach the communication and regulation skills necessary for successful interactions. Individualized relationship supports, like encouragements, acknowledgements, and positive feedback might be the tools allowing this student to gain the needed skills and, therefore, move to the next stage of development.

The needed Tier Two supports, in addition to the Tier One best practices, can be the best "management" approach to minimizing difficulties and thereby, preventing many of those issues we have previously found ourselves reacting to with no specific plan to reach an intended goal. We embed these practices throughout the day in "real time" for teaching, modeling, role-playing, and generalizing until the child is independently able to move beyond his difficulties and continue his growth and development.

Tier Three: Guide

There may still be a very small number of students (one to two per class) who need more frequent and intense support than Tier One and Tier Two can provide alone. Students whose challenges are significantly impacting their social development and learning in a chronic way and across settings will benefit from a Systematic Individualized Intervention Plan for Behavior and Learning.

We must begin with a Functional Behavior and Learning Assessment to discover as much as we can about this student's struggles. We use an inquiry observation approach to gather "data" to understand the function of behavior and to pinpoint the learning obstacles.

A Collaborative Team, including the classroom adults, someone from the leadership team, school director, or level director, support staff, the family, and any community professionals involved with the student, will each contribute to a thorough "observation" and understanding of the student.

After compiling information from each member of the team, a Systematic Individualized Intervention Plan is developed with strategies, techniques, and tools that will teach positive replacement behaviors, provide differentiated instruction, and determine the roles and responsibilities in implementing the plan, monitoring the progress, and making changes to it as needed.

When the plan is fully implemented with fidelity, the student is being supported in making, over time, the changes that will result in success of learning, interactions, and self-regulation skills.

In Conclusion

This is a high-level overview of a Montessori-based Multi-Tiered System of Support for serving most all children in Montessori classrooms and schools, to offer a general idea of how MTSS works and how we can support students with needs in a way consistent with our philosophy and pedagogy. This is a system that can be implemented in any Montessori program and at any level.

As the MTSS framework becomes the norm in education, it is important for the Montessori community to understand its value, benefits, and the ways it can be used in our schools. All educators, both Montessori and non-Montessori, need professional development, consultation, and ongoing coaching to successfully provide for "today's children." Ideally, whoever provides that professional development and coaching will have education and experience in both special education and the Montessori system of education, to best support the development of a school-wide MTSS framework. Educators and school leaders benefit from ongoing embedded positive coaching and consultation with the knowledge, strategies, techniques, and tools to gain the confidence and competence to serve all students in inclusive Montessori classrooms and schools.

CHAPTER 5

Supporting Children with Exceptionalities in an Independent Montessori School

Paul Epstein and Diane Betzolt

Paul Epstein holds a doctorate in cultural anthropology. He has worked in Montessori education for nearly 45 years as an administrator, teacher, school head, teacher education program director, university professor, researcher, consultant, international speaker, and author. He is currently the lead consultant with Designs for Lifelong Learning. Paul presents keynotes at Montessori conferences throughout the world. He is the author of An Observer's Notebook: Learning from Children with the Observation C.O.R.E. *and co-author of* The Montessori Way, *a definitive work on the Montessori experience. Paul writes about inclusion: "We are each a unique expression of life. Our noble task in Montessori is to educate the human potential of each expression. When we don't comprehend a child, adolescent, or adult, we must work to understand so that we can fulfill this task."*

Diane Betzolt holds degrees in elementary and secondary special education, with a concentration in the areas of learning disabilities and social and emotional disorders. She has taught in public and private schools and, for the past 10 years, has been the Resource Specialist at Rochester Montessori School, where she coordinates appropriate instruction between students and guides while also providing support to parents. When asked about her viewpoint on Montessori inclusion, she commented, "As children navigate their way in a Montessori classroom, their learning styles are respected. They are encouraged to build curiosity, confidence, and independence. We look to provide options for students to demonstrate their knowledge in an environment that is nurturing and fosters growth that benefits every learner."

Multi-tiered systems of support (MTSS) offer an array of strategies to children who struggle with learning and behavioral needs. (For more about MTSS, please see Chapter 4, page 44.) MTSS builds on components of Response to Intervention (RtI), a school-wide model designed to support children with academic needs (Harlacher, Sanford & Walker, n.d.; RTI Action Network, n.d.). There are different kinds of RtI models, such as problem-solving, functional assessment, protocol, and blended models (VanDerHeyden, n.d.) Each RtI model incorporates procedures that are used to collect and analyze student achievement or behavioral data, identify learning or behavioral issues, define interventions to address these problems, and evaluate the results of the applied interventions. A common RtI model integrates three tiers or levels, which organize how interventions are designed and implemented (Nellis, 2007; RTI Action Network, n.d.). Different amounts of intervention or support are offered at each tier. A purpose for RtI is to "ensure that students receive early intervention and assistance before falling too far behind their peers" (Fisher & Frey, 2010, p. 16). Consequently, earlier identification and intervention should reduce achievement and behavioral gaps.

The educational principles of RtI and MTSS are similar to those found in Montessori pedagogy. The Montessori curriculum engages children in a hands-on, inquiry-based approach to learning. Montessori guides prepare classroom environments with learning materials. The guides model or demonstrate the use of the materials to individual children or small groups. The guides differentiate their presentations for each child's learning style, interests, and present level of performance. Additional pedagogical goals include supporting children to make independent choices, develop their abilities to concentrate, and become self-disciplined (Seldin & Epstein, 2003). Similarly, RtI models ask classroom guides to identify how each child learns. Guides should differentiate instruction using a variety of methods such as hands-on learning materials and inquiry approaches (Fisher & Frey, 2010; Wiggins & McTighe, 2005).

Building a Response to Intervention Program

This chapter describes the processes and documentation procedures used by Rochester Montessori School (RMS) to identify learning as well as behavioral challenges, set objectives, and monitor progress. RMS is an independent school located in Rochester, Minnesota. Rochester is home to some 130,000 residents, many of whom are immigrants. RMS opened in 1967 as a one-room school for the founders' 3- to 6-year-old children. Today, RMS is located on a 15-acre campus and enrolls over 200 children, from toddlers through eighth graders. Children also study Spanish, the arts, outdoor ecology, and physical education. In addition to its Montessori programs, RMS is authorized by the International Baccalaureate Organization (IB) to offer the IB Middle Years Program to grades six through eight. The school currently serves 19 children with identified disabilities, including ADHD, autism, speech delay, learning disabilities, hearing impairment, visual impairment, and anxiety disorders.

We (Paul, former RMS head of school, and Diane, Resource Specialist at RMS) began building our RtI program during the 2011–2012 school year. We studied several RtI descriptions and resources (for example, Fisher & Frey, 2010; RTI Action Network, n.d.) and decided to build a blended model. This model combines two approaches: problem-solving and a functional assessment. Problem-solving steps include identifying learning and/or behavioral challenges, defining interventions and supports to address identified challenges, implementing planned interventions, and then collecting and analyzing data to assess responses to planned interventions. A functional assessment involves first assessing student performance to establish a baseline. Data is collected and analyzed before providing an intervention (VanDerHeyden, n.d.). The data we collect is identified as a child's "present level of performance."

Following recommendations from Batsche (n.d.), we proceeded by forming a school-wide consensus, developing an infrastructure, writing policies and procedures, and providing ongoing professional development for our faculty.

Build Consensus

We initially identified several issues in our current practices we would need to address in order to build consensus for the implementation of MTSS and RtI. We recognized that we did not think of ourselves as one professional learning community. This was due to several gaps between our Toddler, Children's House, Elementary, and Middle School programs. Some of the gaps were procedural: we needed better documentation of student achievement and readiness for the next program. For example, some of the Elementary guides assumed first-graders coming from the Children's House would be at higher levels of math and reading than they actually were. Other gaps concerned behavioral expectations. For example, some of the Children's House guides had concluded that children who had come from our Toddler program were less independent and less able to concentrate than the children who had not been enrolled in the Toddler program.

Additional issues were personal: several incidents had occurred that resulted in resentment and distrust among faculty. For example, some Children's House guides had received toddlers who required additional services, but the Toddler guides had not shared their concerns. Elementary guides shared similar concerns about the development of children transitioning into their program; they too had received students from the Children's House with unidentified behavioral or academic needs. Several guides said that they had not communicated their concerns because they felt the children would develop and outgrow their challenges. Other guides said they withheld their concerns because they thought the school didn't have effective communication procedures.

To rebuild trust and develop consensus, we began to learn more about one another. We visited each other's classrooms, and we became familiar with one another's developmental and academic goals. Guides shared examples of their curriculum during professional development meetings held during the school year. We shared observed "Montessori Moments"—incidents in which children made a discovery, understood a concept, or spontaneously changed their behavior. "Montessori Moments" include stories about staff members' discoveries and insights (Epstein, 2001). As our meetings became more emotionally safe, we discussed children who were not responding to our core Montessori practices. Instead of judging or blaming one another, we began to regard ourselves as supportive colleagues and think of ourselves as a whole school.

Developing an Infrastructure, Processes, and Procedures

With that hard work underway, we hired Diane as the full-time resource specialist to provide classroom supports and to manage our evolving MTSS and RtI program. We discussed several guiding questions to create procedures for identifying and responding to concerns about children (Nellis, 2007):

- How will we identify children who struggle and need something different?
- What will we use to document this?
- Who will gather this information?
- How, and how often, will we monitor progress?
- Who will use this information and how will it be used?

We developed several procedures in response to these questions (described more fully below). Diane was tasked with managing how we identify and respond to children. During the 2012–2013 school year, we completed an outline of our core Montessori curriculum framework for toddlers through the eighth grade. We used this framework to identify expectations for children moving up from Toddler to Children's House, from Children's House to Elementary, and from Elementary to Middle School. Our work with RtI began during the 2013–2014 school year. We established a child study team made up of guides from our various programs. Led by Diane, the team met monthly to discuss children who may be falling behind, identify possible interventions, and monitor progress (or the lack thereof). Child study members also observed children identified by classroom guides as needing additional support in the Montessori classroom.

The RMS Support Model

Our model consists of three tiers, or levels of support (see Figure 1).

Figure 1: **Three tiers of academic and behavioral support.**

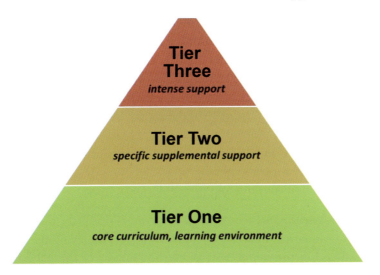

Tier 1: Differentiated Montessori Instruction for <u>All</u> Children

Tier 1 instruction is connected to the school's core Montessori curriculum and the International Baccalaureate units of study for grades six through eight and takes place in the child's Montessori classroom. The RMS Montessori classrooms are prepared environments for multi-age groups of children. Children are grouped as Toddlers (18 months to 3 years), Children's House (2 years 10 months to 6 years), Elementary 1 (6 to 9 years), Elementary 2 (9 to 12 years), and Middle School (12 to 14 years). Each classroom provides a variety of developmentally appropriate learning materials and concrete models of abstract concepts and ideas.

A primary task of the Montessori guide is to observe and understand each child's personality, learning styles, strengths, and challenges (Epstein, 2012). The guides use this knowledge to differentiate instruction. Observation-based instruction occurs when the guide demonstrates the use of learning materials to an individual child or to small groups of children. After a demonstration, children are expected to independently use the material (Seldin & Epstein, 2003). Children typically concentrate when they use the materials. The ability to independently choose and concentrate on the materials is an essential requirement for learning in a Montessori classroom (Lillard, 2005).

Formative Assessments. Classroom guides implement formative assessments using the Montessori three-period lesson model. The first period is an initial presentation or demonstration. Younger children are shown how to use materials. Demonstrations for older children may include an additional challenge, problem, or issue. As children begin to use the materials, the Montessori guide observes and documents what children already know and what they can already do. In the second period, the guide engages children in the inquiry, observing and documenting the learning process. A guide may ask herself: Do children use correct procedures? What are they discovering? What do older children say about their inquiries? Are they beginning to understand concepts correctly? Do they use new vocabulary accurately? What new questions are they asking? Finally, the third period is a summative assessment. The guide collects evidence to assess and document children's new understanding and skills. Evidence could include photographs, classroom tests, completed work, and the child's demonstrations and presentations, to name a few.

Formal Assessments. Formal assessments routinely take place in Elementary classrooms. Reading assessments are given during the beginning, middle, and end of the school year using the Fountas & Pinnell Benchmark Assessment System (Fountas & Pinnell, n.d.). The SRA McGraw Hill Spelling Series is used to assess spelling, and the Sadlier Vocabulary Workshop Series is used to assess and teach vocabulary in the Elementary 2 program. RMS is an authorized International Baccalaureate (I.B.) Middle Years World School. Assessment of Middle School students occurs using I.B. subject rubrics. Finally, standardized testing takes place during the fall and spring for students in grades two through eight, using the Measures of Academic Progress (MAP) assessment program (N.W.E.A., n.d.). Classroom guides will use the school's Initial Concerns/Response to Intervention form (see page 60) if a student's performance falls below expectations.

Behavioral Expectations. Children in a Montessori classroom are also expected to develop self-reliance and social skills. Montessori also identified four phases of independence and concentration through which a child progresses (1917/1991). Guides can use these phases to observe and assess children's progress toward becoming independent and self-reliant.

Tier 2: Additional Interventions for <u>Some</u> Children

Tier 2 interventions are offered to children who score in formal assessments as falling behind and/or have been referred by their classroom guides. Tier 2 interventions include developing additional instructional or behavioral interventions. Depending on the child's needs, the additional interventions may take place in the classroom with the classroom guide or with Diane. Other instructional or behavioral interventions take place out of the classroom and in Diane's room. Diane currently provides additional time for reading, spelling, and math instruction; she works with small groups of two or three children (at all levels) for 25 minutes twice each week. She uses Montessori materials, as well as traditional materials if a child does not respond to the Montessori materials. Diane assists several Elementary children with developing organizational skills. She also leads social skills small groups at all levels to help children with behavioral skills. There are currently five small groups in session, and each group meets once a week for 30 minutes.

RMS Tier 2 Procedures. Our Tier 2 procedures include identifying a child's learning and behavioral needs and challenges, breaking these into smaller measurable components, and defining and applying interventions. We also developed and implemented a data collection and evaluation process, which is used to determine the effectiveness of the interventions and decide if a child can return to the Tier 1 program (Johnson & Pesky, n.d.; Metcalf, n.d.).

Identification begins when the classroom guides complete the school's Initial Concerns/Response to Intervention Form (see page 60). The form is used to describe academic and/or behavioral concerns, and the child's present level of performance. These concerns may have been observed by the guide, identified through assessment scores, or brought to the guide's attention by a parent. The guide reviews this information with Diane. Depending on the situation, they decide on one or more next steps. For example, they may decide to continue to observe and collect data using a Classroom Running Record form (see page 62). Some situations call for first implementing classroom accommodations. Other situations warrant first contacting parents to discuss concerns. In this case, we use a Meeting Summary Log to document discussions, planned next steps, and who attended (see page 64). Alternatively, the guide and Diane may notify the school's child study team and/or notify the head of school to come to the classroom and observe.

When Tier 2 interventions begin, the guide works with Diane and with members of the child study team to complete a Support Log (see page 65).

Specific learning and/or behavioral objectives are recorded. Each objective is tied to the school's curriculum framework and provides a clear focus for instructional or behavioral expectations and achievement. By definition, an objective is measurable and achievable. An objective is an outcome rather than a process and is tied to a specific length of time. For example:

- "During the work period, Jamie will choose one work independently."
- "Sam will independently read three phonetic words each day this week."
- "Brenda will spell 80% of the words correctly during her Friday spelling test."
- "Jackie will work with the guide to complete two division test tube problems in less than 10 minutes daily for the next week."
- "During the next week, Bertha will walk through the classroom and not interfere with another child's work during 65% of the work period."

Strategies used to teach those objectives are identified. For example, the guide may modify the child's work, simplify the steps, model expected behavior, re-present the material, use pictures that illustrate expected behaviors, schedule more practice time, and offer guided practice. Assessment plans are also identified; for example, the guide or resource specialist may time the length of behaviors, record the frequencies of behaviors, take pictures, or check the accuracy of the child's work. The classroom guide, Diane, and child study team meet to review child's progress; they may revise the child's interventions or decide the child no longer requires additional support.

Tier 3: Evaluation and Extensive Intervention for a Few Children

Tiers 2 and 3 differ in terms of the amount of additional instructional time, group size, professional expertise, and the type of individualized instruction (Fisher & Frey, 2010). For example, children receiving Tier 2 interventions may meet with their guides or with Diane once or twice a week; children receiving Tier 3 support may meet daily (Harlacher, Sanford & Walker, n.d.). With parental permission, we work with special educators from our local public school system when a child does not respond positively to Tier 2 interventions. At our request, special educators from the district will observe a child when we have concerns about development. After observing, if warranted, these professionals will administer formal special education diagnostic testing. Based on the results of these tests, a child may be formally recommended for special education services through an Individualized Education Plan meeting to document the child's needs and services, or may be found to be not eligible for special education services. The child may be eligible for a Section 504 plan to accommodate their needs in the classroom. At this time, 10 children from RMS are formally identified as eligible for special education and hold IEPs in partnership with our school district. Based on their IEPs, these children are bused to the local public school, where they receive additional related service for speech therapy and reading and math instruction. Tier 3 students have continued support within the Montessori school setting. Guides are informed of recommended accommodations and interventions to meet the needs of their students within the classroom. Several other children are brought by their parents to other non-public school specialists for speech therapy, social skills development, occupational therapy, and reading and math instruction after the school day. This group of children can be included in receiving special services or may attend for reinforcement of skills.

Tiered Supports in Practice: One Child's Story

Noah (not his real name) is a 7-year-old RMS student. He has been diagnosed with ADHD and fine motor concerns. It is difficult for him to complete his daily work cycle or keep track of his daily materials independently. Noah's guide made observations and recorded the frequency. This data was discussed with Diane. His educational challenges were broken down into smaller steps and each component was addressed with additional instruction and interventions. As we have worked with Noah, we've come up with accommodations to help him be successful. For example, since handwriting is difficult for him, he uses a larger three-sided mechanical pencil, along with a slanted writing easel. This assists with his pencil grip and also limits the pressure that he can use when he writes. Since staying on task is another challenge, Noah keeps track of his daily work schedule (a checklist of four works to accomplish during the school day) on a mini clipboard. When he completes a task, he then checks it off and proceeds to the next. This also assists the guide in keeping track of what Noah needs to focus on at a given time, rather than Noah continually disrupting the class to ask, "What's next?"

Other accommodations that are frequently utilized throughout the day for Noah are headphones to assist in noise control and a wobble seat cushion for assistance in movement. He may choose to sit at the lesson table near his guide and use a folder to hold his daily work. This assists Noah in maintaining his focus and organization.

The use of these accommodations has resulted in Noah being a happy, excited student who continues to learn and is equipped with strategies enabling him to be successful.

Conclusion

The educational components of a tiered model support Montessori pedagogical purposes such as individualized instruction and hands-on, inquiry-based learning. At RMS, we now routinely identify and document academic or behavioral concerns that occur. We are, however, still learning to define academic or behavioral objectives, design and apply interventions, and routinely assess a child's response to the interventions. We are also addressing issues regarding time. Specifically, some of our classroom guides have expressed frustrations that the procedures require too much time to implement, and that this is time taken away from other children who do not require interventions. In response, we continue to monitor and look for ways to simplify our approaches. We also provide support and training to guides in how to write objectives, and we provide suggested interventions (see Suggested Interventions, page 66) and resources to better understand various exceptionalities in their students.

Initial Concerns/Response to Intervention Form

Date   *9/14*
Child's Name   *John*
Age/Grade   *4 years old*
Guide   *Cindy*
Classroom   *Children's House*

1. What is the concern? What are the desired behaviors?

    Concerns: John is unable to sit with work. He is unable to follow directions. He screams "no" when asked to do a work. John becomes aggressive, and he will kick and hit other children. He does not know how to relate to other children; he tries to make friends, but he is too forceful. Desired behavior: John should choose and complete work independently.

2. What is the child's intent? What does the child want or need? (For example, safety and trust, assurances, belonging, autonomy and choice, contribution, fun and play, physical well-being, connection, understanding, peace, order, consistency, purpose.)

    I think he wants to connect socially with other children.

3. With respect to your concern, list examples of what the learner is able to do at this time. (For example, can focus for 10 minutes without assistance. Reads and comprehends at a second-grade level.)

John enjoys being the "leader;" for example, being first in line when we come up from the playground. He can focus on tracing letters in the sand tray. He is not aggressive when we are outside or when he is with two or three other children in the gym. He can make a snack and wash dishes. He can look at a book for 5 minutes. He sits and fully participates in the Spanish group lesson (about five children) for 15 minutes.

Response to Learners (RTL)

4. What is/are your learning and/or behavioral objectives? (For example, "The learner will independently read three phonetic words this week." "During the work period the learner will independently choose two works.")

    John will sit for an entire lesson and then work with the materials independently for 5 minutes each day for one week. John will be in the classroom for the entire morning instead of separating from the class.

5. What strategies will you use to teach these new concepts or behaviors? (For example, modify the work, take out extra steps, model and demonstrate, show with pictures, allow time for practice, offer guided practice, use social stories.)

    We will be consistent in our responses. We will ask John to repeat directions. We will offer a quiet space in the room. We will take out-of-room walks with him. One of us will sit next to him during class gatherings.

6. How will you monitor the new behaviors and document the child's response? (For example, record frequency of occurrence, talk with the child, take pictures.)

    We will observe and time how long he works.

7. For how long will you monitor? (1 day, 1 week, 2 weeks, etc.)

    2 weeks.

8. Please give copies of this form, your monitoring records of the RTL, and meeting records to the resource specialist.

Classroom Running Record

Date/starting time and ending time
9/24   8:35 – 9:30

8:35   John washes his hands, uses the tongs to take snack, and he takes three pieces when Cindy [guide] says "three." He sits at the snack table; he drops to the floor and rolls around. Then he re-sits when Cindy redirects. John brings his dish to the dishwashing station, sets it in the basin.

8:40   John walks to the Farm. He walks past the Farm to the Sensorial shelves. He continues walking, then he sits in chair left of CD player. He bounces in the chair. John walks near me, and he is stamping his feet while walking.

8:42   Cindy directs John to take the Binomial Cube to table. He does. She sets up the lid and box and gets him seated. Cindy leaves John. John builds with the blocks. He doesn't use the lid. He puts the blocks into the box, and he tries to close the box with the pieces "stuffed" in box.

8:47   John is still attempting to get the blocks into box and close box.

8:48   Cindy shows John how to use the lid. She demonstrates and voices, "red touches red." John sorts and places the blocks into box, closes the lid, and returns it to shelf.

8:50   John walks to the classroom doorway where he stands with another child. They wave to children walking down the hall. John stands in front of me, clapping his hands.

8:53   Cindy directs John to the Practical Life area. He sits at the table with the sand activity. He lifts several objects, dropping them back into the sand. He stands, walks back to me, and claps his hands.

8:55   Theresa invites John to walk with her to the office with the attendance form.

8:57   John walks through the room. He stops and watches other children. He continues walking through the room. He chooses a chalkboard and brings it to a table near the window.

9:00   John is running through the room. Theresa [guide] stands in front of John. She asks him to put the chalkboard back on the shelf if he is done. John walks back to the table with it, picks up the chalkboard, and carries it to the shelf. He walks back to the table and pushes in the chair. He walks back to the art shelf and takes an art paper. He walks over to Henry and takes a pen from Henry. Cindy redirects; she tells John that the pen is part of Henry's work. She shows him where to find another pen. Instead, John returns the paper, and then he runs to the coat area.

9:03 John stands next to me. He walks to Alice [student] in the Practical Life area and places his hand on her hair.

9:04 Cindy invites John to help Theresa with packing the classroom bags. He walks over to Theresa and watches.

9:06 John walks over to the math shelf and chooses the teen numbers. He carries the tray to a math table and sits. John randomly hangs bead bars.

9:08 John returns the teen numbers to the shelf. He runs to coat area and squeezes another child's neck. John stops when Cindy intervenes.

9:10 John is marching through the room making loud noises. He accepts an apron from Cindy, and he sits at the clay table.

9:14 John is finished. He takes off the apron, puts it on the table, and pushes in the chair. He chooses a Practical Life pouring activity.

9:17 John stands, and he runs to the clay table where Alice is working.

9:18 Theresa invites John to work with her on washing a table.

9:21 John walks away from the table washing and walks through the room.

9:24 John is pushing another child. Cindy invites John to take a walk with her outside of the classroom.

9:30 John returns to the room with toy objects.

Meeting Summary Log

Date   *10/30*
Student   *John*

Purpose of Meeting

    Review John's classroom progress and review goals and determine if they have been met.

Meeting Summary

    Classroom guides have offered fewer choices. John continues to be impulsive; he usually interrupts other children. He is still unable to focus on an activity for more than 5 minutes. Spanish is the exception—John will participate for the entire 15 minutes. Following directions is still difficult. John goes to the gym daily for gross motor activities, and he is usually able to stay involved with these activities. John enjoys helping.

    The parents share they are changing his diet. John is taking naps in the afternoon. The parents also share that there is a history of ADHD in their family.

Next Steps

    The parents have decided to have John evaluated for ADHD.

Signatures of attendees _____

Support Log

Child's Name *John*
Guide *Cindy*

Date	Concern/Issue	Objectives	Intervention	Response
10/12	Aggressive behavior: kicking children	John will walk through the classroom without kicking others (1 week)	• Redirect • Work with John one-on-one • Give 2-step directions • Give 2 choices • John will wear a weighted vest	• Kicking has lessened • One-on-one redirection works 50% of the time
10/21	Kicking and spitting at other children	John will walk through the classroom without spitting at others (1 week)	• Redirection • Guides model • Work one-on-one • Give two choices • Reduce morning attendance to 1.5 hrs. then build up to full morning	• Kicking and spitting continue 50% of the time • With one-on-one support, kicking and spitting occur 20% of the time
10/30	Sitting in morning gathering	John will sit during morning gathering for up to 5 minutes	• Guide will sit next to John • John will use a weighted vest or weighted lap pad • John will be asked to assist during the gathering	• John sits with the morning gathering for 5 minutes 60% of the time when he uses the weighted vest • John sits for 5 minutes 60% of the time when he is next to the guide
11/15	Same concerns and issues.		• John began medication today.	
11/23				• John is able to choose and complete work. He is not pushing or hitting other children. • We will return to attending a full morning, rather than part of the morning after the Thanksgiving break.

Suggested Interventions (Kindergarten–Eighth Grade)

Organization
- Keep materials in her/his work place
- Written assignment sheets
- 1-2-3 step work plan
- Sit at presentation table
- Written step-by-step directions
- Give directions, have student repeat
- Review planner with guide
- Use organizer folders

Distractions
- Set time limits; use a timer
- Highlight important information
- Work with a "study buddy"
- Work in a quiet area
- Set goals
- Use headphones
- Provide task reminders

Impulsivity
- Describe how she or he should behave when doing a work
- Praise her or him for what is done correctly
- Say the child's name frequently to gain her or his attention
- Use gentle pressure on an arm or shoulder
- Develop and use a reward chart; define specific goals
- Wear a weighted vest; use a lap pad
- Take quiet walks outside of the classroom

Unable to Persist
- Break the work into smaller steps
- Give lots of praise when things are done right and completed
- Encourage the child to do one more step
- Use a timer and slowly extend the amount of time she or he is expected to persist

Choosing and Completing Work
- Use a timer

- Make a visual schedule with pictures of the work sequence
- Name the work and ask the child to repeat the name of the work
- Tell the child what she or he is supposed to do with the work; have the child repeat the description

Social Skills
- Attend social skills group
- Practice effective communication
- Social stories: practice skills and role play
- Reflection
- Attentive listening
- Address student concerns and resolve issues (NVC—nonviolent communication)

Work Quality
- Shorten task
- Address pencil grip
- Use loop scissors
- All staff maintain consistent expectations for accuracy and quality

Reading/Language Arts
- Review vocabulary
- Use directed instruction for phonetics
- Use directed instruction for decoding
- Use directed instruction for comprehension strategies
- Teach how to find key words
- Use guided reading strategies

Math
- Use directed instruction and reteach
- Break task into smaller parts
- Eliminate "extra" materials; use basic materials
- Limit the number of steps, then add more

Processing Information
- Give one direction at a time
- Have the child repeat or paraphrase the direction
- Give concrete examples
- Relate new information to previous experiences and understanding

- Break task into smaller steps; review each step
- Repeat directions
- Restate; clarify
- Write down tasks; write down steps
- Use consistent routines

CHAPTER 6

How Can I Tell Her Parents?

Cathie Perolman

Cathie Perolman holds a Master of Education degree and is a certified reading specialist. Following a 36-year teaching career, she currently works as a teacher-trainer, supports adult learners, and consults in private, public, and charter schools at the Early Childhood (3–6) level. Cathie firmly believes that with the correct training and support for both children and staff, inclusion can truly work and benefit both the child and their community of learners. Her greatest growth has come from knowing and working with children who learn differently, and from guiding classroom teachers and schools to help foster inclusion. The overarching belief in Montessori education that "all children deserve our respect" can indeed serve children who learn and develop other than typically.

In this chapter, I will tell the story of a young child, Marissa (all names have been changed), and me, her 3–6 Montessori guide.[6] I first met Marissa in January; she was 2 years old. Our county holds a yearly Preschool Fair; all the daycare centers and preschools rent table space in a large hall, and families come to see all their childcare choices in one central location. This particular year, our school's table was right next to the door. Marissa's mother approached me, and as I chatted with her about the wonders of the Montessori method, Marissa lay on the floor, her winter coat buttoned up to her chin, screaming at the top of her lungs and kicking the wall. Her mother did not seem fazed by this behavior, glancing over at Marissa only briefly as her screams rose and fell. I had mixed feelings about this. It was 12:45 p.m, and I figured Marissa was hot, hungry, and tired. Once our visit was finished, Marissa's mom picked her up and calmly carried her out of the building, still screaming.

The second time I met Marissa was a week later, at a Saturday morning open house at our school. I felt pretty proud of myself; I thought I had sold

---

[6] Montessorians often use the word *guide* in place of *teacher*, as the adult in the community actually guides the children through the learning rather than actively teaching them. This differentiates the Montessori method from most other classrooms and educational styles.

this family enough on the Montessori method that they were at least willing to come and take a look. Marissa was mesmerized by the classroom. She walked right into the Practical Life area, and got to work taking things off the shelf. However, she clearly needed a significant amount of direction. She took works out but never seemed to really "do" them; she might transfer one spoonful of beans and then walk away, leaving the work on the table. While this is not what we would ultimately want from an incoming student, we were not terribly concerned, given that Marissa was not yet 3 and had never been in school before.

Marissa's parents returned a few weeks later to tour the school and observe the classroom in action. They loved the atmosphere, the structured freedom, and the individualized instruction, and felt strongly that their daughter would thrive in this type of environment. They met with the head of school and completed an application for Marissa to attend beginning the following September. If Marissa was accepted, it was their intention for her to attend the Primary program for the entire 3-year cycle. The family eagerly began reading up on the Montessori method.

Marissa came to the school again that spring for a 30-minute prospective child visit. This visit allows the guide to see how the child separates from their parent, takes direction, selects and works on a task, completes a task, and accepts a lesson chosen by the guide. This also helps our school's admissions department determine if a child is a good fit for the classroom and the school. Marissa, still 2 at this point, was happy to say goodbye to her mom and come with me to the classroom. She was willing to shake my hand (the way we greet children in our school) but did not actually squeeze my hand at all. She made fleeting eye contact, and then her eyes were all over the classroom.

During her visit, Marissa had difficulty focusing. She needed lots of reminders to stay on task and complete a task. She did very little talking; for example, she chose an activity by pointing at it, not by naming it. She was able to complete the puzzle she chose, and, with a reminder, return it to the shelf and push in her chair. She showed interest in the works on the shelf and was able to select just one to do. During the child visit, I try to offer a lesson on a material to see if the child can take direction and accept a lesson. Marissa was openly enthusiastic when I invited her to walk with me to the Sensorial area of the classroom. She did not take my hand, and instead ran on her toes, almost off balance, although she did not fall. I offered her the first Knobless Cylinder block. I showed her how to carry it and offered her the chance to carry it to the table. She just stood silently with her arms at her side. I carried the block to the table, invited her to sit, and said, "First it will be my turn and then it will be your turn. Please put your hands in your lap while you watch." Marissa easily put her hands in her lap and watched me remove two cylinders slowly and dramatically, but then quickly put both hands on the table and pulled out a cylinder with each hand. "Remember, it is my turn first and then it will be your turn. Please put your hands back in your lap," I said calmly as I continued the lesson.

Marissa touched the work twice more before it was her turn. Clearly "watching" a lesson was not an easy skill for this young child. When it was her turn, her work was quick, unordered, and bilateral. She used the "try and stuff" method where she just took a cylinder and tried it in any hole haphazardly until she found one that fit. By the third cylinder she was exhausted and ready to quit. She needed significant attention and support to complete this work, and it did not seem to be very fun or fulfilling for her. The lesson ended with Marissa and me taking turns putting the cylinders back.

After the prospective visit, I met with our school's admission director about my time with Marissa. I shared that she was enthusiastic, eager to try activities, and able to follow directions with prompting. I also said that she took a significant amount of adult attention, and she was never able to work on a task independently during her entire visit. I noted that I wished I had taken each Knobbed Cylinder out and placed it in front of its corresponding hole instead of having Marissa take the cylinders out herself and try and place them properly. It is always a tough call at those first meetings; I never want to underestimate the ability of a child. I thought that Marissa possibly had some red flags for focus issues and other motor and developmental issues.

Montessori schools are great places for children with special needs, but the key is not to have too many children in the same class who need additional supports, in order to allow the class to normalize. If a parent knows a child has special needs, the admission department needs to get that information and pass it on to the guide so he or she is as prepared as possible. In many cases, however, new children are "wild cards" and they may have issues that adults are not aware of before the children enter school.

The admission director felt that despite the red flags I noted, Marissa had 3 more months to mature and develop some impulse control before September, when school began. She was encouraged that Marissa's parents had followed the admissions protocol so well—taking time to observe a classroom and read about the Montessori philosophy. She felt the family was an excellent match for our school. Ultimately, Marissa was accepted and would start that fall.

Before the start of each school year, I make a phone call to new parents, inviting them to come with their child for a meet-and-greet session. During that phone call I take the time to chat a bit and get to know the parents. I ask if there is anything I should know about their child—food allergies, fears, special needs, favorite colors, etc. I spoke to Marissa's mom, Julie, on the phone and she was delighted to talk to me. She said Marissa was afraid of dogs and did not like soft food. She loved purple, and to run and be outside. She felt Marissa was a happy-go-lucky child who would be a great match for Montessori, and that she and Marissa's dad, Tom, were so happy that she got a spot in our school. We arranged a time for the meet-and-greet, and I ended the conversation by saying that I was looking forward to getting to know Marissa and their entire family better (Marissa also had a baby sister). During this phone call I also make a point to say to parents that I want this year to be a great year for their child and their family, and that I am available to talk with them about whatever they might need. "Please feel free to contact me if you need to." I give them the phone number and e-mail addresses that are appropriate to use, and encourage them to contact me if they have any concerns or questions. This phone call sets the tone for an open and honest relationship.

In the last week of August, Marissa came for a 15- to 20-minute meet-and-greet session. During this meeting, the family gets to see the class set up for the school year, and the child gets to find their cubby, meet our class fish, fill their extra clothes box, see the bathroom, and even try out the toilets if they want. That day, Marissa was not her enthusiastic, happy-go-lucky self. She wore her swimsuit cover-up zipped all the way up to her neck with the hood over her head, even though it was a very warm day. She insisted on wearing flip-flops and tripped in them; she cried many times during her visit. Her parents were visibly disturbed and embarrassed. Julie explained that they had just gotten home from vacation the night before, they were not unpacked yet, and no one had slept well the night before. Marissa was not interested in anything in the classroom except the fish tank. She was totally unwilling to even consider using the bathroom. We assured her parents that every child is entitled to a rough day, and sent them on their way with encouragement and smiles. So Marissa could form a happy memory of school, we had them exit through the playground. We still had a long weekend before school started.

Our school year begins with a phase-in period of 3 days when only the children new to the class attend. This gives my assistant and me a smaller adult/child ratio and allows us the chance to get to know the new children. We give them a lot of lessons so they have choices of work and develop a solid groundwork for a work cycle (take a work from the shelf, do the activity, then return it to the shelf) by the time the rest of the class joins us the following week. During the phase-in period, the new children get to know each other and start to create the beginnings of a community. These days are typically shorter than our usual mornings and do not include lunch.

On the first phase-in day, Marissa came to school with her dad, arriving right at 8:55 a.m. She shook hands with me and gave her dad a half hug goodbye. There was no evidence of the behavior she displayed in the meet-and-greet a few days before. I led her to her cubby, where she put her sunglasses away, and then easily joined the children and Miss Alissa, our assistant, who was reading a story. Marissa sat and appeared to listen, although her eyes wandered all over the room, taking everything in. We then had our very first circle time where we sang each other's names, looked at the calendar, learned to roll and unroll a rug, saw a few basic Practical Life works as a group, and then went to work.

Marissa chose to sit at a table by herself and work on the same puzzle she had selected at her prospective child visit. She needed reminders to actually do the work as well as to finish it and put it away. Selecting the next work was difficult. There were quite a number of new children, so Marissa could not have the undivided attention of a guide. The next time I looked over, she had three works out. I helped her select one of them and put the others away, noting to myself that one of the adults in the classroom needed to stay aware of Marissa and help her establish her work cycle. During the morning, she moved often, frequently leaving one work out and quickly going to another. However, she put her work away and came to group snack when asked. She was quite reluctant to wash her hands before snack, but with encouragement she finally did swish her hands through the water, and we let that count. She stayed for more small group lessons and appeared interested in them.

We invited Marissa to use the bathroom during the second work time and she was not at all interested. I worried she might have an accident. For the rest of the work time, she appeared to be happy and engaged, and that was positive from our point of view. We ended our classroom morning with one last circle where we sang a few songs. It was clear that Marissa found this difficult and was noticeably uncomfortable. She covered her ears, her eyes got big and round, and she said, "No! No! No!" I was not sure if she was tired, did not like our songs, did not like singing in general, or found the singing too loud.

During our playground time, though, she was in her glory. She loved to run and kept moving the entire time we were outside. She tried out all of the climbing equipment and had a big smile on her face. The difference in her facial expression outside from how it had been inside made me think that school had been quite challenging for her. I had not been aware of that while we were in the classroom, but it was quite obvious now.

After the playground, it was time for pickup. Marissa was all smiles, and Julie asked me how her morning was. I answered honestly that she had had a good morning. I knew the importance of building a strong trusting relationship with Marissa's parents as we got to know and understand her.

As phase-in week continued, and we had more of a chance to work with and observe Marissa, several issues came to light. She vehemently avoided the bathroom at school. This apparently made for a lot of screaming and crying on the way home, and several near-accidents. Julie called me as soon as they got home that first day to tell me how difficult the ride home had been. I explained that Marissa had been invited to the bathroom three different times and had refused to even enter the bathroom. We agreed that a parent would accompany her into the bathroom at drop-off time as well as at pickup time; however, Marissa would have no part of the classroom bathroom. During the day, we invited her to use the bathroom both individually and as part of a small group, but she was also unwilling to even come into the bathroom. Her parents assured us that she was totally toilet-trained at home. We felt certain that this was just an issue of familiarity with the school bathroom. Once she got used to school, she would use the bathroom here as well as at she did home. Starting the next week, she would be staying longer days and she would have to use the bathroom.

Marissa seldom really "did" a work. She often took an activity off the shelf and just worked with it, but did not complete it. It was hard to know where she was in the process of the work. There was still the distraction of the new room and the other children, and Marissa was still new to the whole idea of school.

Some work was hard for her. For example, Marissa disliked playdough. Most 3-year-olds love the feel of playdough, and I thought she would really enjoy that lesson. However, she physically recoiled when I took it out and showed it to her; she was not even willing to touch it.

Marissa showed little interest in other children. She did not make any effort to work with them or to socialize with them. Julie always asked her at pickup time who she played with, and Marissa never answered. She still used very little verbal language, but we were getting better at figuring out what she wanted and needed. We were getting the hang of each other, and all in all we felt we were learning to learn together.

The next week, the rest of the children in the class returned, and Marissa continued to find her way. She was somewhat overwhelmed by the older children and her work cycle did not develop easily. While the returning children were initially kind and supportive, they clearly found her challenging and began coming to me with reports. "Miss Cathie, Marissa has two works out again!" "She has pieces of the puzzle all over the floor and on the table and on the snack counter." "Marissa has had that work all morning and I have been waiting and waiting for it." I encouraged them to help her learn the ways of the classroom and reminded them of how the older children helped them when they were just beginners.

September melted into October, and we saw little change. We made a point of having an adult nearby and always helping Marissa define when a work was finished. She could "muck around" in a work all morning and never really know when it was finished. So we made it our "adult work" to define for her when a work was finished, hoping that she would come to know when she had reached that point herself. We also hoped this would give her a chance to explore more works in the classroom and open herself up to new learning opportunities. (At this point, she was only doing a few of the same works over and over again.)

Marissa stayed at school all day and napped after lunch. She continued to struggle with all aspects of hand washing and using the bathroom. While Marissa really did want to have snack during the morning work time, the expectation that she wash her hands prior to eating was too much for her to handle. In mid-September, we began having individual snack: each child chose snack as they would any other work in the classroom. The child found his special name card and placed it on the snack table to reserve his place, and then went to wash his hands. He got his snack, brought it back to the table, and began eating. Once he was finished eating, he cleaned up his crumbs, washed his place mat, and replaced his snack name card in the "finished" basket, indicating that he had already had his snack.

Marissa needed help with all aspects of snack, as did many of the youngest members of our community, but she regularly bypassed the hand washing step. She either just ate without washing her hands, or, if the other children were adamant and insisted that she wash, she just wet her hands, moving just a few fingers through the running water and drying them as quickly as possible. When I watched her, it seemed almost painful for her to have the water touch her hands. This was going to become a bigger and bigger challenge as the cold and flu season set in, when we start requiring children to wash hands as they enter the building as well as before snack and lunch.

After watching this for a week or so, I talked to Marissa one-on-one about her challenges with hand washing. I asked her if there was anything I could do to help make hand washing easier for her. I had wondered if she found it scary to put her hand under running water, so I had shown her the Montessori hand washing exercise, in which she placed each hand in a basin of still water to wet it. This was not any better received. Marissa was not able to share any thoughts with me, and her eyes or body language gave me no clues either. I was disappointed: I had so hoped that getting the issue out into the open might help her realize that we could find a solution together.

I wrote her parents an email and asked how they handled hand washing at home. The next day at drop-off, Julie told me it had been a difficult night at home. She said they usually just grabbed Marissa and tickled her as she walked by, and then used a baby wipe to wipe her hands while she fussed and strained. "Sometimes you just have to pick your battles!" she said. I wondered if I should decide that this was not a battle worth fighting either. Should I get a box of baby wipes and teach Marissa to clean her hands using these? Was that the right thing to do to teach this child a level of independence? I made a note to myself to check if that was indeed a sanitary practice, and if so, if other children in my class might want that option also.

The bathroom also remained an issue. Marissa had begun to enter the bathroom with the other children by late September but it was clearly difficult for her. Some days she was willing to sit on the toilet but often she just refused to even pull down her pants. As a result, Julie and Tom were the frequent recipient of wet clothes at the end of the day. Early in the year, Julie had emailed us to ask us to put Marissa in a pull-up diaper at nap time, saying that is what she wore at home. Although this was not common practice in our school, we had done it before when appropriate for a child; in this case, we agreed for the sake of Marissa's morale.

Marissa's communication was also concerning. She was talking a bit more, but her sentences were often repetitions of what she had just heard me or Miss Alissa say, or something she had heard on television, rather than her own original thoughts. I made a point to greet her warmly every day and make a comment on her clothing. She started to use that as a way to connect; every morning, she would say something to me about her shirt, usually, "I wore this shirt to school today." Then I would reply by commenting about the color or the pattern. It was a start!

She was following our routines better, and she seemed more and more comfortable in our classroom, demonstrating a generally calmer demeanor. She even had found a buddy—she always sat next to Chelsea. They did not really converse, but they seemed to enjoy being in proximity to each other, and they ran around after each other when we went outside. And isn't that the first step in making a friend?

Alissa and I began to collect our thoughts by discussing each child in depth. Six weeks of school had passed, and our class was fairly normalized. Formal parent conferences to discuss the children's progress were in 3 weeks, and both Alissa and I would be present, so it was important that we were aligned in our thinking on each child. Alissa was experienced and had excellent insight as well as a love for children; I welcomed her perceptions and valued her wisdom. When the two of us sat down to discuss Marissa, we noted the following:

- Marissa does not use the bathroom at school—she has accidents or urinates in her pull-up, even though her parents say she uses the bathroom at home. But she had urinated in the toilet at school twice. Was that luck or progress?
- Marissa refuses to wash hands at school. She is physically uncomfortable getting her hands wet to wash them or to do any kind of water work/washing work at school.
- At the age of 3, Marissa has very little expressive language. She speaks, but it is mostly to mimic what she has heard.
- Marissa does not like songs or singing, and covers her ears during singing time.
- Although Marissa chooses work and does interact with materials, she does not complete work without guide involvement.
- Marissa loves being outside and enjoys running for long periods of time. She toe-walks.
- Marissa has the very beginnings of her first friendship, but it does not include any interactive language.

Having noted all these concerns, I wondered if I should call Marissa's parents in for a conference before the scheduled formal conferences. It was a difficult decision to make. Generally, I would say that more communication is better than less communication. When I invite the parents in for a separate conference, I am saying that I want to share my thoughts about their child. In this case, I had been sharing thoughts over the course of the 6 weeks Marissa had been in school. I'd already discussed Marissa's ongoing challenges with the bathroom, the decision to use pull-ups at nap time, the way her parents cleaned her hands at home, and her reticence to wash hands at school. But all the conversations had been short and about a single subject. The conference would be a more formal time to address broader questions. I hoped Marissa's parents already saw me and Alissa as caring, supportive members of Marissa's life who were helping her develop to her optimal potential.

Nonetheless, I'd still have to proceed with enormous care and compassion, because Marissa's parents might be on guard. I decided to discuss this with my head of school and possibly with another mentor or guide at school. Eventually, I decided to invite Marissa's parents in for a conference before the regularly scheduled conference time. I didn't want to wait until the first week in November, but rather hoped to begin to address some of her issues and move the process forward. (While we have regularly scheduled conferences, we don't want a "progress conference" to be the first time we bring up concerns. Although we don't do formal assessments, we are always aware of the children who are performing other than typically. We want to be proactive in our concerns and seek help sooner rather than later.)

As the conference approached, my thought process went as follows: "I don't know these parents very well so I will have to take my lead from them. I will encourage them to share their thoughts. I am trying to understand their views about Marissa and her development. Are they at all concerned? What, if anything, has been said to them in the past? My goal of this conference is not necessarily to refer Marissa for an evaluation, but to understand her parents' views and to perhaps plant the seeds for a future evaluation. I am building my trust with them and doing some serious, conscientious parent education. I could start the conference like this: *Thank you so much for coming in. We are so enjoying getting to know Marissa. She certainly loves the playground and is an enthusiastic runner. She has a lot of energy and can run for a very long time.*

"I will open with positive statements about Marissa. Now I will ask them a question. *What is Marissa saying about school?* That will give me some insight into what she shares at home. Perhaps she does not have much language at home either. They may not realize what level of language is typical at this age. *Who is Marissa talking about?* This will give me more insights into her language development as well as her social development. Remember, this is their oldest child. They have possibly never seen other 3-year-olds play before and they may have no idea what typical 3-year-old play might/should look like. *How do you think the transition to school has gone?*

"This is also their first experience with school for their child. They are learning so much about what school is and what the routines are. They have only been part of the community for 6 short weeks. *What is Marissa's language like at home? What does she talk about? Does she carry on interactive conversations with you? Have you ever had concerns about her language? Has your pediatrician ever expressed concerns about it?* If they tell me Marissa is not talking at home except to repeat what they say, I will need to recommend that they schedule an evaluation as soon as possible. I will need to have referral information ready. So I need to have a plan in my mind. Every county in the United States has Child Find, which is a free service through public schools that provides developmental evaluations for preschoolers."

"I can ask the parents, *What can we do to help Marissa with using the bathroom at school? What can we do to help Marissa with hand washing at school? Are you working on teaching her traditional hand washing with the faucet and soap?* Sometimes I am pleasantly surprised with the amount of support a child is already receiving. But often the parents are unaware of the child's challenges and I am the first person who has brought these concerns to their attention. It is not unusual for a parent to be unable to process my concerns the first time they hear them. That is why I try to raise my concerns multiple times before suggesting an evaluation. However, I do not want the family to leave the meeting without an action plan to proactively address some of Marissa's issues. We want to help her feel comfortable and be as successful as possible in every aspect of school."

"I can say, *These are the things we are doing to help Marissa grow in her ability to handle the expectations of school.*

- *We are going to allow her to wear a pull-up at nap, but we are going to ask that she sit on the potty each time we ask her. We will ask you to have her sit on the potty at drop-off also to give the school potty some family credibility. Do you think that seems like a reasonable expectation for Marissa? She has already said that she likes the one closest to the door so that is the one she can use. We will wait until it is available. Can you talk to her about it and remind her about this each day?*

- *We are going to ask her to put her hands in the water and count to two. In time we will increase the time she keeps her hands in the water. Is that asking too much? What do you think?*

"Based on the conversation that transpires during the conference, I will help the family understand that we are working together to help Marissa. If at all possible, I will mention that I may in the future recommend that we look outside of the school for help in supporting Marissa. I call this 'planting the seed' for needing an evaluation."

We scheduled the first conference for right after school, when Marissa could be part of the aftercare program and her younger sister could be in care also, so the parents could focus on our conversation. However, as it turned out, only Julie was able to come, and she looked frazzled and exhausted. She explained it had been hard to get away from work early, that the baby had been sick, and this was her first day back to work since the baby's illness.

We began the conference. Julie said that Marissa was very happy at school. She doesn't talk too much about school or the children at school but Julie could tell she was happy in her classroom. Yes, she talks all the time at home, she said. As a matter of fact, she knows lots and lots of songs and nursery rhymes, and she sings and says them all the time. When I tried to ask about Marissa's level of interactive language, Julie did not really seem to know what I was talking about and grew a bit anxious and uncomfortable. I decided not to press the matter.

Julie talked about Marissa's use of the potty at home. As she talked, it became clear that Marissa was using the bathroom more on a schedule rather than expressing her own bodily needs. Marissa had a little potty of her own and that is the only one she would use. Julie admitted that Marissa did not use the bathroom in public places, with one exception at a Target store. "But we are working on it," she said proudly.

The conversation about hand washing was a more detailed version of the conversation we had had previously. Julie said that Marissa really hates getting her hands or any part of her body wet, so they used baby wipes and did the best they can. I sympathized that baths must be difficult, and she sighed and nodded. I asked if she had discussed these things with their pediatrician, and she explained that due to her husband's change in employment, they had not had a consistent pediatrician. In fact, Marissa had not yet had her 3-year-old checkup; they were looking for a new pediatrician that works with their current insurance plan.

I voiced my concerns and the items I hoped to work on actively at school. Although Julie seemed surprised, she was willing to go along with the plan to have Marissa sit on the potty every day at drop-off and each time the children use the bathroom (before playground, after lunch, after nap, etc.), and to wet her hands and count "one, two," as a step toward soap-and-water hand washing. I asked Julie to talk to Marissa about these things at home as well so she knew that we are all working on them, and Julie agreed.

Next, I mentioned that most children entering the class were toileting and hand washing independently, and that was our goal for Marissa as well. I also mentioned that there are professionals who could help us if these things were not successful. (I worried that this comment might feel threatening to Julie; I meant it to feel supportive, so I said it with as much kindness and compassion as I could.) Julie seemed to take it in stride, and so I was hopeful that I had planted yet another seed about a recommendation for an evaluation that I suspected I would have to make in the future. I thanked Julie for coming and sharing so generously about Marissa and her family. I encouraged her to find a pediatrician and offered to share a list of pediatricians that other parents in the school had used and liked.

Before Julie left, I invited her to our "share your class" morning early the next month. This is a special morning in which parents come to school with their children and for half an hour, they can watch the children do their work. I shared that this event often helped families gain insights into how their children develop and learn in a Montessori classroom. Finally, I explained that we would meet again in a few weeks for our regular progress conference the second week of November.

In late October, Julie got an opportunity to see Marissa as part of the class when she chaperoned our yearly pumpkin patch trip. On this day, Julie was responsible for Marissa as well as a 4-year-old and a 5-year-old classmate. We rode the bus, took a hay ride, picked pumpkins, fed the animals, and generally had a fun outdoor fall morning. Marissa found many parts of the trip overwhelming, and needed her mom to carry her and encourage her much of the morning. She covered her ears when the other children were squealing with delight as the hay wagon went through a muddy riverbed. She didn't like having to step over the pumpkin vines, and stopped and cried. She recoiled at the animals and would not even go near them, much less consider feeding them. The hay maze was fun for her, perhaps because the trail was flat and the route predictable. Throughout the day, I wondered if Julie noticed the differences between her daughter and the other 3-year-olds in the class.

In early November, Julie came to the first "share your class" morning. Marissa was eager to show her mom her class. She took out her favorite work, the puzzle, and removed just five of the eight pieces, then replaced three of them. Then she removed two more and replaced three. She then took out four more and put one more in. Julie then handed her the pieces, one by one, until the puzzle was complete. I heard Julie ask Marissa about other children working nearby, but Marissa did not name any of them, nor did she talk to them. I was aware of lots of spontaneous conversation going on between other 3-year-olds and their parents, and again I wondered how it felt to Julie that her child was not participating in any of that.

Throughout the fall, our plan to have Marissa sit on the potty daily was a partial success. Due to the scheduled nature of these attempts, there were some successes, and we celebrated them both with Marissa and with emails to her parents. However, Marissa's own awareness of her bodily need to go to the bathroom did not increase, although the number of accidents and bags of soiled clothes decreased, so that was positive. But if the adults in the environment forgot to tell Marissa to use the bathroom, or if the toilet closest to the door was not available, there was usually an accident.

Our success with hand washing was not successful at all. Marissa really tried, but it was just so difficult for her that she avoided it at all costs, hiding when it was hand washing time. It became a battle. As a Montessorian, the first rule in Dr. Montessori's *Decalogue* is "Do not touch a child unless invited, whether explicit or implied" (AMI, 2005). I was not going to force her, even though cajoling her just did not work. We quickly regressed to a fast swipe of a few fingers under the water; that was really the best she could do.

New challenges cropped up. Marissa crowded other children on the circle and in line when walking to the playground. She did not seem to know how much space her body took up, and we were constantly helping her find the "bubble of air" on each side of her when she was sitting on the circle. Older children avoided sitting next to her.

Later in November, both Julie and Tom were able to attend Marissa's regularly-scheduled progress conference. We began by sharing that Marissa was following the routines of school with ease: she put her work away when the bell rang, lined up after the playground time, sat on the circle, etc. Her parents told me that Marissa followed the home routines well too, unless one of her rules was broken. I asked them to explain this, and they said that, for example, if they accidentally put her pull-up on backward, there could be an hour-long tantrum. Another long tantrum could ensue if, after putting Marissa in bed, one parent tucked her in with the lines on the blanket horizontally instead of vertically. I asked, "Why does she not just ask for those things to be fixed?" Julie and Tom looked at each other, and Tom said, "She does not know how." He explained that she did not ask for anything with more than one or two words, and instead usually just pointed to or cried for what she wanted.

"Of course now we know most of what she wants, so we just give it to her, but during 'meltdown time,' we have no idea what is wrong."

"It would really help if she had some language, wouldn't it?" I asked.

"When do you think that will come?" Julie responded, as tears rolled down her cheeks.

"I think it might be something worth exploring with a professional," I replied.

We went on to talk about other things that Marissa was doing in the classroom—the kinds of activities she chose in the Practical Life, Art, and Sensorial areas. Julie commented that Marissa could not really complete the puzzle without help at the "share your class" morning, and I added that Marissa did have difficulty completing work, though she seemed to find work interesting and was always eager to try activities. Her parents asked when she would learn to read, and I explained that it was a progression: Marissa needed many readiness skills first, and we needed to strengthen her oral language skills first as well as her hand for writing.

I steered the discussion back to Marissa's language, and explained that Child Find was a free service through the public school system that offered developmental screening. The first step would be for the parents and the school to fill out paperwork, after which an observation and referral could be scheduled. I encouraged Julie and Tom to contact Child Find to start the process, and I let them know I would be happy to fill out any necessary paperwork. I explained the various ways it could work: in some cases a therapist would come to the school and help me learn how best to work with a child. In other cases, children received services at a neighborhood school. I explained that, because a child's brain is more malleable at a younger age, early intervention is key and can yield more quick and valuable results.

These words were all difficult to say. Each time I say these words to parents, I find them challenging to say. Before these types of conferences, I practice saying the words I will use. Usually I phrase the words and practice the conversation in my mind. Once I feel that I have it right, I begin rehearsing it aloud in my car until I can get the words out easily enough when I am in front of parents.

Tom and Julie were hard to read. On one hand, they looked relieved, and on the other, a little shell-shocked and sad. I gave them a paper that I had prepared with the contact information about our local Child Find services. Finally, I closed the conference with some positive words. I thanked Tom and Julie for coming, and told them I would do my best to answer any questions they might have after they had time to think about our conference. I encouraged them to take their time processing all that we had talked about, and let them know I realized that it was a lot of information. I also emphasized how much we were enjoying getting to know Marissa, and that we looked forward to seeing her bright and ready for school each day.

The very next day, Julie called Child Find, and within a week I had the paperwork to fill out. A few weeks later, Marissa had an initial appointment with Child Find. Her screening indicated a need for further assessment in the areas of language, academic, and fine-motor development. She had further assessments with a speech-language pathologist, a special educator, and a pediatric occupational therapist. Her family also found a developmental pediatrician (a pediatrician with special training in identifying a range of developmental and behavioral differences).

Marissa continues to attend our Montessori school. Julie, Tom, Alissa, and I continue to work together to find ways for Marissa to strengthen her language skills, fine motor skills, toileting skills, and academic skills. She is receiving some support services outside of school, and we are receiving some guidance from those outside professionals as well on how to best support her in the classroom. This team approach has been highly successful in helping Marissa be successful and grow optimally! We continue to meet regularly with Julie and Tom to ensure that Marissa's program is working for her.

It is the primary role of a guide to create strong, caring relationships with families. These personal connections help families be more able to hear us when we need to share difficult information with them. Remember, you are not expected to know about all types of exceptionalities, or to be able to diagnose children with these conditions; this is a very complicated field that encompasses many professionals and levels of expertise. You are just the guide on the path to getting an accurate referral for a child who needs it. That is the initial and often the most important step! Some families will want to discuss the details of the process with you as they go through it, and others will not want to share at all. But either way, you will know that you have made a significant difference in the life of a child.

Steps for a Successful First Referral Conference

A referral conference is often the first time a guide shares concerns about a child's progress that they believe should warrant a referral for an evaluation. This conversation can be difficult for both the guide and family members, and should be addressed with great sensitivity. The following steps can provide a framework for a strong, positive relationship with families so the referral conference goes smoothly.

1. Create a warm relationship with the parents and the child.
2. Observe, observe, observe.
3. Make modifications based on your observations.
4. Share information generously with the parents. Be sure to celebrate the positive.
5. Speak kindly and gently to parents, acknowledging the child's challenges and your modifications. Look to them for ideas and possible solutions.
6. Invite your head of school or another experienced guide at your level to observe if you are unsure of your thoughts about a child.
7. Schedule the conference at the convenience of the parents.
8. Plan your message and your exact words. Rehearse. If you are unsure of how to say what you need to say, ask a more experienced teacher to help you phrase your message.
9. Prepare for your conference. Have tissues available. Begin with a positive statement about the child. Share the child's challenges, and explain that you would like to get more information through a referral. Explain that professionals with expertise in the areas of concern can help both you and the family know how to work with their child better.
10. Have the referral information readily available so you can hand it to the parents. Thank the parents for coming and make it clear that you are happy to help in any way you can: filling out paperwork, answering questions of other professionals, and allowing other professionals to come to the classroom and observe the child. Assure the parents that you are willing to meet again if they would like. Sometimes it takes more than one conference for this information to be clear for a family.

11. End the conference on a positive note, telling the family how much you enjoy their child and how much they add to the community.

CHAPTER 7

Montessori Teacher Supports for Children with Exceptionalities

Ann Epstein

Ann Epstein holds a doctorate in early childhood special education and is an associate professor at the University of Wisconsin–La Crosse. Ann loved teaching at the Primary level in public and independent Montessori schools for 15 years, and has served as a Montessori teacher educator for nearly 40 years. Montessori's deep commitment to honoring and respecting each learner's individual potential drives Ann's current work. This enduring respect guides how we support and nurture every learner. It is a shining example of how Montessori can support children who learn and grow a bit differently. (This chapter was originally published in Montessori Leadership *(volume 21, issue 2, 2019, pp. 6-13).* Montessori Leadership *is the official magazine of the International Montessori Council.)*

Supports for children who have special needs and attend public school programs have been legally mandated for several decades in the United States. The Individuals with Disabilities Education Act (IDEA, 2004) became law in 1990 and was updated in 2004. Public schools must provide Individualized Education Programs (IEPs) for students with documented needs that meet IDEA's specified criteria. IEPs identify needed accommodations, special education services, and supplementary aids as well as their frequency and duration. Montessori guides who teach in public school settings typically collaborate with special educators and service providers (for example, occupational therapists) to provide appropriate services for children who have exceptionalities. Children who attend independent Montessori schools are also entitled to federally supported services allocated through local education agencies (LEAs). LEAs are usually housed within a school district's special education program.

In addition to accommodations (services and supplementary aids specified in children's IEPs), Montessori guides in both private and public schools often need to adjust classroom practices. Depending on each child's individual needs and strengths, adjustments can affect how guides teach lessons, demonstrate materials, design the classroom environment, assist children during transitions, facilitate conflicts, and address a myriad of other day-to-day interactions. This chapter provides examples of how Montessori guides support children with exceptionalities in Primary (ages 3–6) and Lower Elementary (ages 6–9) classrooms. Supports address Montessori developmental aims of concentration, independence, and order, as well as fine and gross motor skills, cognition, and social/emotional growth.

Some guides and administrators hold the view that adjusting classic presentations or changing aspects of the work period conflict with their training and are "not Montessori." However, changes can make the difference between a child being a successful, joyful learner or being frustrated and even miserable. The following recommendations are either current evidence-based practices, or have been suggested by Montessori guides experienced in working with children who have exceptionalities. Each guide and school head needs to decide if these suggestions fit with their view of Dr. Montessori's philosophy. It is my hope that these strategies will offer possible solutions and perhaps expand the Montessori community's view of what it means to follow each individual child's learning path.

Practical Life experiences such as mopping bring a sense of accomplishment, self-worth and pride, essential for children who are building social connections.

Observation, Present Level of Performance, and Goal Setting

Before examining specific supports for learners with exceptionalities, attention must be given to determining the child's strengths and needs. Dr. Montessori implored teachers to observe children carefully (Montessori, 1909/1964). Though Montessori stated that "…the teacher shall observe whether the child interests himself in the object, how he is interested in it, for how long, etc., even noticing the expression on his face…" (1909/1964, pp. 108–109), she did not provide specific observational formats. Rather, she emphasized the importance of both capturing details of how children work with materials and honoring "principles of liberty" (1909/1964, p. 109). Montessori warned against insisting a child pursue an activity, noting this can cloud whether or not the child is truly ready to engage in exploring and learning specific concepts.

Montessori and current special education practices both value the importance of documenting the child's present level of performance. Anecdotal records (brief objective snapshot statements of a child's performance), running records (more in-depth accounts of how a child carries out an activity or an interaction), and checklists (noting whether a child carried out a particular activity or behavioral expectation) are all helpful. The aim is to document as much detail as possible regarding the child's current level of understanding and/or behavior.

If, for example, a guide is concerned that a 3-year-old child concentrates for short periods of time, documenting the start and stop times of the child working with various materials can provide helpful data. The guide may learn that the child spends more time with Practical Life activities and less with Sensorial materials. The guide could further note whether the child concentrates longer when working with a peer, if there are differences in the child's concentration at the beginning of the work period vs. the middle or the end, and if the child sustains attention for longer periods of time when playing outdoors. Careful observations and documentation will assist guides in determining, in as much detail as possible, the child's present level of concentration.

Once the child's present level of performance (sometimes referred to as PLOP) has been clarified through the observations noted above, guides may find it helpful to compare it to developmentally appropriate expectations. The American Academy of Pediatrics (n.d.) partners with Healthychildren.org to provide expected milestones in the areas of movement, fine and gross motor skills, language, cognition, and social and emotional development. Using the above example, perhaps the guide notes that the child does not consistently follow three-part commands nor can recall parts of a story. This could suggest the child is having difficulty understanding verbal explanations and reminders, leading to another round of observations.

The Center for Disease Control (CDC) also provides information regarding expected milestones in a resource titled "Learn the Signs–Act Early." When Montessori guides wonder if a child is "on track" in any developmental domain, it is helpful to refer to several recent, professionally vetted milestones. Milestone ranges can be useful guidelines for children birth through age 6, given that teachers' as well as parents' expectations can be either high or low.

Lower Elementary guides may find academic standards helpful. State departments of education provide expectations in language arts and math for each grade level, as does the Common Core (n.d.). While the Montessori curriculum does not align completely with traditional reading, writing, and math expectations, guides can use academic standards to better understand a child's level of performance. Both the National Center for Montessori Education in the Public Sector (public-montessori.org, n.d.) and the Association Montessori Internationale (amiusa.org, n.d.) provide suggestions for aligning Montessori with elementary standards.

The final—and crucial—step in determining a child's present level of performance is to fully accept it. Guides truly need to be at peace with a child who, for example, works with an activity for an average of 3 minutes across settings, times of the day, and with or without peers. Supporting this child in increasing his or her concentration occurs much more easily if teachers are not resisting the child's current length of time. Thinking, "Jane just can't concentrate. How can I manage our classroom when Jane only concentrates for 3 minutes?!" adds stress for both the guide and the learner. Alternatively, accepting what the child *can* currently do—consistently focus for 3 minutes—is more likely to result in planning for and then implementing a successful change. Once the learner's PLOP is clearly documented, the guide shares this evidence of the child's learning with parents. A portfolio of photos, videos, and work samples helps families understand what the child is able to do and where the child is struggling. Again, it is important to consider the *range* of ages between which children reach milestones. For example, it is typical for children to produce clear /r/ sounds in their expressive speech any time between age 3 and (particularly for boys) age 7. At this point, parents often benefit by observing the classroom, not only to perhaps catch a glimpse of the concern, but to view the range of skills across age levels.

Next, goal setting is carried out with families. Before meeting with a family, the guide drafts a manageable, achievable goal, and reflects on possible interventions. At the meeting, the guide can share possible approaches and recommendations, and also invite families to share their own ideas, including changes that could support the child at home as well. The goal can then be adjusted to fit the family's needs and priorities. Working in respectful partnership is essential to the child's success. Once everyone has agreed on a clear plan, it is helpful to document it, whether with a quick text, an email, or a simple hard copy. Ongoing, frequent communication between families and guides is especially important if a goal needs to be altered once interventions are implemented.

Montessori provides all children with meaningful opportunities to move from concrete representations of complex concepts such as time, to abstract representations. This is particularly important for children who struggle with processing information.

Strengthening Concentration

The previous example addressed helping a 3-year-old child increase the average length of time working with an activity. It is important to note that according to IDEA criteria, difficulty concentrating in and of itself is not considered a special need. However, it is often a component of a language disorder, an intellectual disability, or even an emotional disorder. And difficulty focusing on a task or activity can "simply" be associated with a child's temperament.

Perhaps the family and guide agree that concentrating for 5 minutes (on average) is an achievable goal for the child. The guide had observed that the child stayed with an activity longer as the morning work period progressed. However, arrival, settling in, and choosing an initial activity appeared to be particularly difficult. The guide also observed that the child enjoyed the book reading area of the classroom and often looked at books for up to 5 minutes. The guide suggested (and the family agreed) that either the guide or assistant and the child would read a story together at the beginning of the work period. The child would select the story, and they would read for at least 2 minutes. The adult would then lead the child to either the Practical Life or Sensorial area, offer the child two choices (for example, a Knobbed Cylinder block or the demonstration tray of the Geometric Cabinet), and gently remind the child to complete the work before returning it to the shelf.

Several components of a potentially successful outcome are present in this scenario.

1. Beginning the work period with adult support with a preferred activity (story reading)
2. Making a choice between two specific preferred activities (rather than choosing from the whole array of activities in Practical Life or Sensorial)
3. Listening to a gentle reminder of expected behavior (complete either the demo tray or the cylinder block before returning it to the shelf)

Supports for children in Lower Elementary classrooms who struggle with concentration issues can be tailored to their developmental levels. For example, 6- to 9-year-olds are typically able to monitor their own time with a personal watch or a classroom clock. Often, they enjoy "beating their time" by seeing if they can concentrate for an additional 5 minutes. Lower Elementary students are also able to use "self-talk" more effectively than younger children. For example, reading or reciting a statement like the following can be helpful:

"I am learning to focus longer and longer on my work. Today I am aiming for 15 minutes. I know I can do it!"

Lower Elementary students also enjoy visual displays of their progress. Guides can assist them in making their own daily and weekly graphs that show the number of minutes they focused successfully on their work. Guides can either send families a hard copy or an electronic file of the learner's graph each evening.

Rochester Montessori School (Rochester, MN) Lower Elementary guide Andy Sawyer stated his single most effective support for students working to stay focused has been offering an opportunity to run several laps around the school soccer field first thing in the morning.

> Over half of the students in my class took advantage of our offer and ran four or five laps, if the weather cooperated. This provided social time as well as a way to wake up their brains (synapse activation). It really did help everyone begin their day ready to learn. (A. Sawyer, personal communication, July 2016).

Other ideas for both Early Childhood and Lower Elementary include transferring weighted balls, walking the line while holding a weighted object, window washing, and gardening tasks (e.g., digging, watering, or planting). These activities all allow children to move with resistance, and the proprioceptive input aids children in achieving and maintaining a "calm-alert state" (Luborsky, 2017, p. 315). Guides may consider creating a nonslip, padded "jump spot" (Luborsky, 2017, pp. 332–333) where children can hop or jump. A designated yoga area in the classroom, containing headsets that play soft music and cards depicting child-appropriate poses, can also help children find and keep their inner sense of calm.

Effective supports can be as simple as noise-canceling (or white noise) headphones. Children who only stay focused for brief amounts of time can then enjoy and attend to books and other learning activities for longer periods of time.

Table 1 (below) notes supports that could prove helpful for children in Montessori Primary and Lower Elementary classrooms who are working to strengthen concentration. As with all learning in Montessori environments, careful observation is required to discern if a particular support matches an individual child's needs and strengths.

Table 1. **Supports for children working to increase concentration**

- Movement opportunities before work period: outside play, running in gym or commons area (for example, play "chase" with an adult or peer), yoga station
- Noise-canceling headphones
- "Office" carrels for Lower Elementary (partitions that decrease visual stimulation and distraction)
- Child's own dedicated work space (individual table or floor space)
- Timer or hourglass
- Exercise ball in place of chair (Lower Elementary), standing desk or table
- Work period breaks (drink water, have a snack, take note to classroom nearby or to office, observe classroom pet)
- Sensory breaks (select item for exploration: rain stick, snow globe, bean bag)
- Puppet break (helpful for children with strong social needs)
- Padded non-slide jump cushions, stationary bike, low balance beam

Encouraging Independence

Montessori (1909/1967) recognized the child's inner drive to carry out tasks without adult assistance. She urged guides (and parents) to refrain from "helping" children with any task or activity children could carry out on their own. Montessori also designed each learning material with an inherent control of error, eliminating the need for an adult to check or correct children's work.

Occasionally, children need support in carrying out procedures independently. Photo booklets, similar in design to Social Stories™ (Gray, 2004) can be helpful. If, for example, a child has difficulty remembering each of the steps involved with using the restroom, a guide can display sequential photos on the bathroom wall. Sequential photos can also assist children who struggle with putting on and taking off snow clothes, as well as cleaning up after lunch, or putting away work and joining classmates for a community gathering. Please see Figure 1 (below) for example of a social story regarding appropriate touch.

Figure 1. **Social story to assist child having difficulty with personal space.** (livingwellwithautism.com)

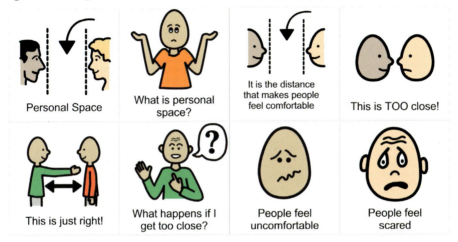

Assisting Development of Children's Sense of Order and Self-Discipline

Early Childhood educators assist children in learning to regulate their behaviors and develop self-discipline (de la Riva & Ryan, 2015). Montessori addressed a component of self-discipline by recognizing the importance of respecting children's sense of order. She noted that, "Order is one of the needs of life which, when it is satisfied, produces a real happiness" (Montessori, 1936/1966, p. 52). Montessori believed that children have an inner sense of order that is nurtured when their surroundings and routines are predictable, consistent, and orderly. If this is so, and children are still not able to regulate their behaviors, guides may need to provide additional supports.

Strategies regarding multisensory integration can prove effective in helping children manage their behaviors and, ultimately, develop self-discipline. While not formally recognized by the U.S. Department of Education (2015) as a special need, difficulty integrating sensory input can result in learning and behavioral challenges. Recently termed "sensory processing disorder" (SPD), difficulties include unsteady balance, hyposensitivity or hypersensitivity to touch (children can be hypo or hyper in various different situations throughout the day), fine motor weakness, and poor muscle tone or coordination (Sensory Processing Disorder, n.d.). Occupational therapists typically provide services for children with SPD. There is controversy regarding the effectiveness of SPD strategies; however, occupational therapists (Sweet, 2010), special educators, and pediatricians note successful outcomes (Gourley, Wind, Hennigher, & Chinitz, 2013; Noddings, 2017). Montessorians have found success helping children regulate their behaviors (for example, impulsively touching, shoving, or hitting a peer) by calming themselves through the use of weighted lap pads (in Early Childhood classrooms) and therapy balls (with Lower Elementary students) for short periods of time. The use of sensory integration materials and equipment should be supervised by a knowledgeable professional (for example, a special educator serving as a consultant to a Montessori school).

Practical Life and art activities such as pouring rice or water, working with play dough, and hand washing (perhaps with the option of applying a small bit of lotion) can help young children with challenging behaviors develop self-discipline. The length of the activity is a key point. Guides may need to shorten long works (those with several steps, such as polishing or dish washing) so children working to regulate their behaviors can be successful. Reducing the number of steps provides them with the opportunity to repeat soothing steps and not lose track of what to do next. For example, table scrubbing can be modified to include only dampening a small brush, running it over a bar of soap, scrubbing, and then drying the table with a hand towel. This allows children to repeat circular scrubbing strokes over and over, often bringing them to a calm state. Providing a variety of interesting items to scrub (large seashells, car tires, or large pumpkins) and modifying the number of steps can provide children with successful self-regulation experiences that also honor and strengthen their sense of order.

Both Primary and Lower Elementary guides may find it helpful to design a small area of the classroom (or even a single shelf) to house sensory items. Rain sticks, soft hand puppets, snow globes, unlit scented candles, scented hand lotion, headphones that play nature sounds, and kaleidoscopes can provide relaxing sensory input. Children can have the option of selecting one of these items and "taking a sensory break" for a specified amount of time. Or several items can be placed in a basket for children to select, take to a rug or table, and then explore as they would any other material.

Teaching young children to use specific verbalizations can also help develop self-regulation. Rochester Montessori School Resource Specialist Diane Betzolt describes her success in working with a highly active 3-year-old.

I had worked with Sam for around a month, modeling slow movements and quiet voice levels. We worked on puzzles and read stories together in my classroom (resource room) several times a week. I also modeled the phrase, "I am calming my body" while we pursued various activities. One day, Sam's teacher brought him to my room for an unscheduled work time. Sam had been running in his classroom and was unable to focus on any activities. Red-faced and a bit out of breath, he declared, "Miss Diane, I calming my body!" While I modeled taking a slow, deep breath, Sam repeated this phrase and did calm his body. We worked together for just another few minutes until he was ready to return to his classroom. I reminded his teacher to use this strategy with him. She later shared that modeling and encouraging Sam to calm his body were effective. (D. Betzolt, personal communication, July 2016)

Similarly, Lower Elementary children may have success repeating self-affirmations. Coupled with taking one or two deep breaths, using phrases such as "I can be calm again" or "I feel myself calming down" can help learners return to a calm state. Guides can remind children to use these statements when necessary.

Supports for Strengthening Motor Skills, Cognition and Memory, and Social/Emotional Skills

Children with exceptionalities in specific developmental areas, such as speech and language, may have services documented on their IEP. Often, though, Montessori guides observe the need for supports within and across developmental domains before IEPs are developed. Fine motor supports can take the form of pencil grips and adaptive scissors. Attaching magnets to three-part cards and providing a magnetic white board (or a simple aluminum cookie sheet) can offer security to a child with weak eye-hand coordination. Time riding on stationary bikes (child-sized), jumping on mini-trampolines, and walking across very low balance beams (4 to 6 inches off the floor; children remove shoes and socks) can help children strengthen and coordinate large muscles. In addition, these activities often help children develop order, concentration, and independence.

A wide array of strategies is available to Montessori guides working with children who struggle to remember information. Reflection approaches such as SQ4R (Hartlep & Forsyth, 2000) can help children remember specific concepts and definitions. Guides can model the components—survey, question, read, recite, write, review—or tailor the strategy to suit individual children. Self-talk (repeating definitions to oneself) and mnemonic devices can be helpful. Graphic organizers, from standard Venn diagrams to fish skeletons (Figure 2, below), can assist children in understanding and remembering overlapping characteristics and relationships, including cause and effect and "if/then" relationships. These visual organizers are particularly helpful for learners with specific learning disabilities related to writing. For example, a child in Lower Elementary struggling with character analysis might identify "impatient" as a character's trait. If asked to connect character traits with events in the story, the child might realize that the character spilled a magic potion. The Montessori guide could ask the child to list traits above the horizontal line (the backbone of the fish) and note corresponding events below the line.

Figure 2: **Fish skeleton graphic organizer** (www.slideshare.net):

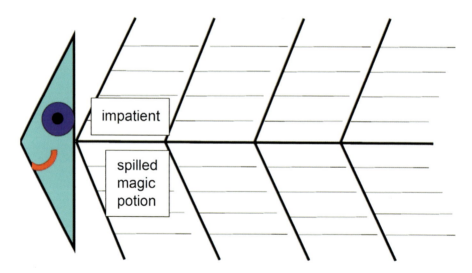

Dr. Montessori identified effective cognitive strategies that have withstood the test of time while working with children who struggled with early reading, writing, and math concepts (Montessori, 1914/1965). She modeled a multisensory approach by showing children how to gently stroke sandpaper letters while repeating their sounds (/a/, /a/, /a/). Guides can offer children similar opportunities with puff paint as well as felt letters and numerals. Tracing letters in farina or cornmeal sprinkled on a tray or over ziplock bags filled with hair gel offer additional tactile experiences.

Currently, three main types of trauma have been identified (the National Child Traumatic Stress Network, n.d.):

Acute	Chronic	Complex
A single event that lasts for a limited amount of time.	Multiple events, often over a long period of time.	Exposure to varied and multiple traumatic events, often of an invasive, interpersonal nature.

A fourth category, developmental trauma, is being considered and pertains specifically to complex trauma experienced by children in early childhood. According to Sar (2011, p. 2):

> Developmental trauma refers to a type of stressful event that occurs repeatedly and cumulatively, usually over a period of time, and within specific relationships and contexts (Courtois, 2004). Childhood abuse (sexual, emotional, and physical) and neglect (physical and emotional) constitute typical forms of chronic traumatization.

Leaders in the field of trauma are working diligently to advocate for this classification because it would allow research and professionals to formally address the fact that adverse childhood experiences and complex trauma experienced in early years require a different framework of support than cases of trauma that are experienced later in life.

The CDC-Kaiser Permanente Adverse Childhood Experiences (ACE) Study, conducted between 1995 and 1997, studied more than 17,000 adults and found a highly significant correlation between adverse childhood experiences and adult mental health disorders, heart disease, cancer, skeletal fractures, and other major illnesses (cdc.gov). The study questioned adult HMO members about adverse childhood experiences such as abuse, neglect, and family dysfunction. The results were alarming and indicated that adverse childhood experiences are significantly more prevalent than previously appreciated or documented.

In the study, 30.1% of responding adults reported physical abuse, 23.5% reported being exposed to family alcohol abuse, 19.9% reported exposure to sexual abuse, and 18.8% reported they were exposed to mental illness. Additionally, 12.5% witnessed their mothers being battered, 11% reported having been emotionally abused as a child, and 4.9% reported drug abuse within their family. The findings also suggested that an individual who experiences significant adverse childhood experiences will be more likely in later life to experience symptoms of depression, alcoholism, suicide attempts, drug abuse, sexual promiscuity and sexually transmitted diseases, domestic violence, cigarette smoking, obesity, and sedentary lifestyles.

In our Montessori community, we witness the effects of trauma firsthand in our schools and classrooms. Children affected by child traumatic stress are those who, well after the traumatic event or events, experience emotional and physical responses that interfere with their daily living. Even though the threat may no longer be present, these children may continue to be triggered by things that they sense, see, hear, remember, feel, or smell that remind their bodies of the original danger. Some symptoms may include:

> ... intense and ongoing emotional upset, depressive symptoms or anxiety, behavioral changes, difficulties with self-regulation, problems relating to others or forming attachments, regression or loss of previously acquired skills, attention and academic difficulties, nightmares, difficulty sleeping and eating, and physical symptoms, such as aches and pains. Older children may use drugs or alcohol, behave in risky ways, or engage in unhealthy sexual activity. (NCTSN, n.d).

Please keep in mind that not all children exposed to danger will develop traumatic stress. The brain has a set of crucial neural networks that mediate stress response. When children have attentive caregiving at home and supported emotional, motor, social, and cognitive experiences throughout their early years, they develop a well-regulated stress-response system. This leads to experiences in learning and growth that shape a child in positive ways. (Perry, 2016, p. 28)

Below is a diagram that illustrates the different stress responses in the body:

Positive Stress	Tolerable Stress	Toxic Stress
Considered normal and essential. Examples: A shot at the doctor, or the first day of school.	Serious, temporary stress responses, buffered by supportive relationships. Examples: Losing a family member or sustaining a bad injury.	Prolonged activation of stress response systems in the absences of protective relationship. Examples: Exposure to violence or chronic neglect.

Perhaps the most effective cognitive support is careful error analysis followed by modeling and guided practice. Where does the learner become confused? If a Primary-aged child cannot follow all the steps of dynamic addition, the guide can return to static addition and re-teach the process more slowly. If a silent demonstration is not effective, verbalize the steps. "I have eleven unit beads. I will exchange ten of my beads for a ten bar. Now I have one ten bar and one unit bead." The guide should ask the child to repeat her actions and verbalization, and then stay with the child as he practices. This assistance should continue for several days, and the guide should only step back when the child demonstrates understanding. Scaffolding instruction (Berk & Winsler, 1995) is important for all learners but often critical for children who struggle with cognitive processing.

Supporting children who are upset, frustrated, and perhaps even aggressive can be particularly wearing for Montessori guides. Just as math and literacy skills need to be modeled, social skills must be overtly taught for some children. Grace and Courtesy[7] lessons typically include inviting a peer to work together, passing in front of another ("excuse me"), and waiting for a busy teacher's attention (placing one's hand on a guide's shoulder). Addressing one's own strong emotions and learning to resolve conflicts require step-by-step demonstrations, followed by opportunities for practice. These practice lessons should take place with a willing peer when both children are calm. When an actual upset occurs, guides need to calmly step in and remind children of each step.

For example, if a child (Mattie) appears to kick another child's (Sara) Pink Tower, the guide first helps the kicking child identify intentions and feelings. "Are you mad at Sara?" "Would you like to work with Sara?" "Are you upset that Sara did not ask you to build the tower with her?" Then the guide asks Sara to share her feelings. "How did you feel when Mattie kicked over your tower?" Once feelings and intentions are identified, the guide facilitates a resolution. "What do you think we should do now?" Guides are often surprised at how quickly children offer a next step. Occasionally children need ideas, but resolution is much more effective if it is generated by participants rather than by the guide.

Again, the critical component of providing supports for children who struggle with social and emotional challenges is that guides must teach these

---

[7] "In Montessori schools, children are formally instructed in social skills they will use throughout their lives, for example, saying "please" and "thank you," interrupting conversations politely, requesting rather than demanding.

skills directly. Just as lessons are given to help children learn rhyming words and subtraction, guides need to demonstrate and then help children practice and learn conflict resolution. That said, the design of the learning environment could assist in fostering a peaceful atmosphere. Inviting work areas with small lamps, gentle miniature waterfalls, soft fabric wall hangings, quiet music, and aromatherapy suffusions add soothing sights, sounds, textures, and smells to classrooms.

Dr. Montessori began her pedagogical work with children who did not learn easily. Over 100 years later, Montessori guides continue her legacy of providing individualized instruction. Whether children have IEPs with specific services or are in the grey area of "struggling learners," Montessori guides have both the opportunity and responsibility to provide assistance. Once the child's level of performance is determined, a plethora of supports are available. In collaboration with families and specialists, strategies can be carefully selected, implemented, and monitored. If the child does not achieve the targeted goal, another support can be implemented. Throughout this process, guides are indeed adhering to Dr. Montessori's original directive to respect and honor each individual child's strength and areas of need (Lillard, 1972; Montessori, 1909/1964).

CHAPTER 8

Montessori as a Safe Haven for Childhood Trauma

Maria Eva Chaffin and Brynn Rangel

Maria Eva Chaffin, MSE, is currently conducting research for her doctorate in organizational leadership in autism and Montessori. She holds master's degrees in exceptional student education and business education, a bachelor's degree in special education, and is AMS-credentialed (Early Childhood). Originally from Venezuela, she has over 20 years of international teaching experience, and it is her life's passion to work with children with special needs. With her background in special needs and her Montessori credential, she is convinced that the Montessori method is the best way for all children to learn.

Brynn Rangel is proud to be part of the Montessori community both as a parent and a professional. She is a Board Certified and Licensed Behavior Analyst, and has been working with individuals with varying exceptionalities, families, schools, and organizations since 2006. She specializes in implementing positive behavior support strategies and behavioral management systems for schools and organizations around the world. Brynn also holds a master's degree in business administration and was the executive director of a non-profit school and therapeutic center for children with autism and related exceptionalities. Brynn's view of Montessori inclusion: "Montessori nurtures the whole child and celebrates each student's unique strengths. Through love, careful observation and goals that honor the journey of each child, Montessori educators can meet the needs of all learners.

> The discovery that the child has a mind able to absorb on its own account produces a revolution in education. We can now understand easily why the first period in human development, in which character is formed, is the most important. ~ Maria Montessori (1949/1967, p. 28)
>
> Fear destroys curiosity and playfulness. In order to have a healthy society we must raise children who can safely play and learn. There can be no growth without curiosity and no adaptability without being able to explore, through trial and error, who you are and what matters to you. ~ Bessel van der Kolk (2015, p. 352)

Your heart is breaking, and you feel lost. Johnnie's tantrums are inconsolable and getting worse. Isabella flinches every time someone comes too close to her. Kate shuts down or becomes angry every time you give her positive feedback. Ziare is falling asleep in class and his parents are reporting that he is awakened many nights with nightmares. Christina struggles to focus. What is going on? How can you help?

While there are a variety of reasons that we may see behavioral challenges in our students, a conversation about trauma is one that our community must embrace. When we think about trauma, our minds often jump to cases of abuse, neglect, school shootings, violence and war, or natural disasters. While these are real and valid, we also must include in our conversation other factors that we may not automatically consider. It is important to understand that even though adults may work tirelessly to protect children, trauma can result from factors such as the loss of a loved one, severe illnesses or medical procedures, exposure to people with mental health or substance abuse disorders, caregivers with histories of trauma, epigenetics, and more.

Epigenetics is an interesting and relatively new field of interest with respect to the long-term effects of trauma. Epigenetics is the study of a phenomenon and "the mechanisms that turn on and off the expression of our genes without altering the DNA sequence" (Franco, 2018, n.d.). One could consider that epigenetics encompasses the practical and useful changes to the function of a gene without actually changing the structure or sequence of the gene. Although epigenetic changes are not uncommon in nature, childhood trauma, among other stressful life events, can trigger epigenetical changes that impact the expression or function of genes.

The National Child Traumatic Stress Network (n.d.) defines a traumatic event as "a frightening, dangerous, or violent event that poses a threat to a child's life or bodily integrity" (https://www.nctsn.org). It is also important to know that a child can be traumatized by witnessing a loved one's safety being threatened—because children develop their sense of safety from how safe they perceive their caregivers to be. As Dr. Maria Montessori wrote in *The Absorbent Mind*, "Children have many kinds of sensitivity, but they are all alike in their sensitivity to trauma" (1949/1967, p. 131).

Toxic stress creates an overactive stress response in the body and brain. This over-activation then causes our biological systems (which are designed to identify danger and signal our bodies to fight, run, or freeze) to break down or become overresponsive. It is imperative that we understand that traumatic stress reactions are not choices that our children make when coping with trauma. They did not choose the beautiful balance originally constructed within their brain biology to be disrupted to the point of dysregulation. Thus, they need our empathy and our help. As caregivers and educators, we can create safe spaces where our children can work to restore their inner balance and teach our students the tools and skills needed to cope with their trauma and regulate their feelings.

Montessori as a Safe Place to Heal Trauma

> The immense influence that education can exert through children has the environment for its instrument, for the child absorbs his environment, takes everything from it, and incarnates it in himself. With his unlimited possibilities, he can well be transformer of humanity, just as he is its creator. The child brings us a great hope and a new vision. (Montessori, 1949/1967, p. 66)

Trauma can feel like an overwhelming topic. How are we supposed to help these children? What if we haven't received specific training in this area? How do we identify and meet the needs of the children who need us most?

Luckily, we are more equipped than we may realize. Part of identifying what each child needs as a unique learner is recognizing that children may have histories or symptoms of trauma. Dr. Maria Montessori observed the effects of trauma on children, and her findings are reported in her research. It is incredible to see that her discoveries from many years ago align with what current researchers and professionals are working on today. Montessori's discoveries are embedded in her pedagogy and call us, as Montessori educators, to be understanding and sensitive to the effects of trauma and needs of the developing brain.

One of the prominent current experts and researchers on the subject of childhood trauma is Dr. Bruce Perry. Perry is a psychiatrist, and currently a Senior Fellow at the Child Trauma Academy in Texas and an adjunct professor of psychiatry and behavioral sciences at the Feinberg School of Medicine in Chicago. Dr. Perry is the co-author of the bestselling book *The Boy Who Was Raised as a Dog*. He has garnered a world-renowned reputation for his work on the social, behavioral, emotional, cognitive, and physiological effects of trauma on both children and adults. His research has been influential in understanding the epigenetic and biological changes that occur in the brain as a result of childhood trauma.

Montessori can be a place of healing for all children. Maria Montessori created a method that directly addresses critical areas of development, including those that may be affected or disrupted in children experiencing trauma. Montessori requires the cultivation of safe, loving, nurturing relationships and environments to meet the needs of students. This is exactly what traumatized children need: a safe place to heal. When you work with children who have experienced trauma, one of the most important ways that caregivers can help is by building positive relationships. Perry (2016, p. 2) noted that "within this inner circle of intimate relationships, we are bonded to each other with 'emotional glue'—bonded with love." Maria Montessori said, "Of all things, love is the most potent" (1949/1967, p. 295).

In order to be ready to build positive relationships with students, Montessori requires teachers to prepare themselves physically, emotionally, and spiritually. Montessori talks about the importance of the spiritual preparation of the teacher. This is a deeply meaningful concept that calls the teacher to be calm and at peace with herself in order to best show love, peace, and calm to the children.

> The real preparation for education is a study of one's self. The training of the teacher who is to help life is something far more than the learning of ideas. It includes the training of character; it is a preparation of the spirit. (Montessori, 1967, p. 131).

Preparing ourselves in this way is critical for all children who we work with. However, it is even more important for children who have experienced trauma and "will be in a persistent state of alarm and less capable of concentrating… and will pay more attention to the nonverbal cues of a teacher, such as tone of voice, body posture, and facial expressions" (Perry, 2016, p. 28).

Another tool that Montessori teachers possess that can help these children is observation. In her article "The Scientist in the Classroom: The Montessori Teacher as Scientist," Ginni Sackett expressed, "Our legacy as practitioners of Montessori education is not the legacy of an educator: It is the legacy of a scientist. Montessori came to this work as a scientist and she remained first and foremost a scientist until the end" (2016, p. 9). Montessori directs the teacher to use the scientific method to observe the children, to learn about each one individually and discover each child's specific needs. Teachers are called to be protectors of the children and help each child entrusted to their care to grow and develop socially, emotionally, and academically.

> Our work is not to teach, but to help the absorbent mind in its work of development. How marvelous it would be if by our help, if by an intelligent treatment of the child, if by understanding the needs of his physical life and by feeding his intellect, we could prolong the period of functioning of the absorbent mind! (Montessori, 1949/1967, p. 28)

The environment also plays a critical role in helping our students affected by trauma. By cultivating a safe and nurturing environment where each child's unique needs are acknowledged, children can grow in confidence and self-esteem. The Montessori environment allows for movement and is optimal for the development and regulation of physical, emotional, and intellectual systems. "Mental development must be connected with movement and be dependent on it. It is vital that educational theory and practice should become informed by this idea" (Montessori, 1949/1967, p. 141). In addition, Montessori recognizes the importance of independence and embraces children working at their own pace. Traumatized children can be allowed to explore and excel at a rate that works for them.

Many times, victims of trauma are not ready to meet academic demands. Thus, providing order and the opportunity to practice life skills (through the lessons of Practical Life and Grace and Courtesy) is critical in the healing journey. Montessori teaches these things alongside academics and shows students how to be a member of a community. Taking the time to teach conflict resolution and emotional regulation is part of nurturing the whole child. It also helps those struggling in these areas to regain what was lost or could not be learned before. The heart of Montessori recognizes that each child is a masterpiece and provides students, especially those healing from trauma, what they need most: to be seen through the eyes of potential and celebrated for who they are. "Understanding trauma is not just about acquiring knowledge. It's about changing the way you view the world" (Bloom, 2012). Yes, it requires a change in our perspective, in our paradigms—we must see the world through a different lens. Yet this is the way that Maria Montessori viewed children. Without judgment, we must see their needs and become guides to help them unlock their potential.

Here are some examples of Montessori as a safe haven.

Lucy

Lucy was a Primary student exhibiting aggressive behaviors towards her peers. Her teachers reported that she was also taking classroom materials and other students' personal items home with her. Lucy's parents reported they were not seeing any of the same behaviors at home and that Lucy was experiencing typical cognitive, social, and emotional development. To work with the family and try to improve Lucy's behavior, Lucy was moved to a different Primary classroom.

At first, Lucy did not engage in the same problematic behaviors. However, once she became comfortable with her new peers and environment, the new teaching team began to observe Lucy taking objects from the classroom without permission and acting aggressively towards the other students. The new teaching team decided to meet and talk extensively with her parents. They learned that Lucy's mom had a history of severe trauma and was coping with a mental health disorder, and that Lucy's parents were living in different states and struggling to co-parent. What was once assumed to be a child "behaving poorly" was now identified as a child affected by trauma.

Being open-minded and accepting of Lucy and her family, the school team decided to strategize to help her. They worked with the parents, and decided to let Lucy take home one object a day from the classroom to share at home and then return the next day, in hopes that this would eliminate the stealing behavior. Her team further identified that the function of Lucy's aggressive behavior was to gain attention. Therefore, they started giving Lucy individualized attention and teaching her how to gain attention appropriately from her peers. Grace and Courtesy lessons about trust and appropriate play were also integrated. It took time, patience and love, but Lucy's behavior improved dramatically over the course of 3 months. After that, if the teachers observed any of the old behaviors, they took them as a cue to provide more attention and revisit any necessary lessons or communication skills.

Thomas

Thomas was an Upper Elementary student who had been in the foster care system for most of his life. Most recently, he had been placed in a very loving and consistent home, with caregivers who were committed to his well-being. Many outside services and resources were in place, and Thomas was a becoming a flourishing member of his Montessori community.

Then one day Thomas ran out of music class and back to his classroom teachers, and wouldn't say why. Everyone tried to talk to Thomas about this, but he couldn't find words to describe why he left. It seemed to be an isolated incident, until it wasn't. He periodically started to leave classrooms and seek out other staff members without permission. The school became very concerned and considered this behavior to be a safety issue. Thomas's foster parents were afraid that he would be asked to leave the school.

Upon closer observation, the team was able to identify a pattern: Thomas was only leaving class on days when there was a substitute teacher. The teaching team decided to ask Thomas which three staff members he had the best relationships with, and then asked those staff if they would be willing to have Thomas visit their classes when a substitute was scheduled. Once agreed, the staff let Thomas know that he could ask appropriately to go to one of the available, agreed-upon staff members any time there was a substitute teacher. The school honored the fact that Thomas was not yet able to trust or build relationships quickly with new people. As an alternative, they gave him the permission to make safe and appropriate choices, and he stopped running out of class.

As Montessorians, we need to understand the importance of preparation, building relationships, and accepting each child as an individual; these are fundamental requirements to effectively work with and help children with trauma develop improved self-reliance and resilience. To achieve these goals, Montessori teachers must focus on personal connections and relationships that help children develop trust, feel safe, and ultimately progress towards healing and recovering from traumatic experiences. Through these connections, trust, and healing, children can better connect to the classroom environment and material while developing the social and emotional skills needed to grasp and understand fundamental Montessori principles such as Grace and Courtesy. We must never underestimate the importance of avoiding our preconceptions of behavioral cause, but instead focus on observation as a mechanism to identify behavioral and environmental patterns that allow us to better understand the "root why" or source of behavior. A normalized and highly functional Montessori classroom and environment has all the tools necessary to help heal childhood trauma and recognize and view the child as a whole individual, and not merely a student with bad behavior.

CHAPTER 9

Trauma-Informed Montessori

Colleen Wilkinson

Colleen Wilkinson is an AMS-credentialed teacher (Early Childhood), teacher educator, consultant, and a director at Montessori Country Day School in Houston, Texas. She lives with her wife, teenage daughter, and many pets. She is passionate about trauma-informed care, anti-bias/anti-racist (ABAR) work, adoption and foster care, and disability rights. She serves on the American Montessori Society Peace and Social Justice Committee, and in her local school district, is a member of the Special Education Parent Advisory Committee and District Education Improvement Committee. In addition to her partnership with trauma-informed care and social justice organizations, she provides professional development and support groups for parents and educators. She says, "The most important aspect of a Montessori classroom isn't the Pink Tower or the Colored Bead Stair, it is the relationship you have with each and every one of your students."

When I became a parent in 2009, it quickly became apparent to me that both the ways in which I was raised, and the positive discipline approach I had used for years as a classroom teacher, were going to be insufficient. Becoming a parent to a 7-year-old who had spent most of her first plane of development in foster care required a different and intentional parenting style. I scoured the internet, joined support groups, reached out to wise sages of the adoption community, and begged for guidance. I was told that a relational approach, described as therapeutic parenting, was the way to proceed. I learned the concepts and implemented the ideas. I was thrilled when it went well, devastated when I made mistakes, and encouraged by my daughter's clearly growing healthy attachment style. I found other parents striving to embrace and maintain a therapeutic parenting style, and we created online and in-person support networks for parents. These networks have supported me when I needed guidance, and celebrated with me when my child hit trauma-specific milestones. (Your local Mommy group just doesn't share the same kind of joy when you are so excited that your child threw away food for the first time after years of supporting them through a food scarcity fear.)

School presented a challenge. In my support groups, I heard a common refrain: "My child's teacher does *not* get it," often followed by a chorus of, "Teachers won't listen to me!" In fact, I felt the same way. I didn't feel much sympathy for the teacher who called me to report that her arm had been slammed in a door as she attempted to take my child's lunchbox away. My response was, "Did you read my email explaining food scarcity? You triggered her deepest fears." I guarantee this was not the response this adult expected. Teachers were often perplexed at my lack of willingness to "punish" behavior that, to me, was clearly a manifestation of a trauma response. I was perplexed by the school's rigidity and refusal to adapt to the needs of my child. The benefit of my Montessori training was a deep belief in the power of observation, a willingness to follow the child, and a desire to see the need behind the behavior. The urgent need to support my child rid me of any dogmatic rigidity about one methodology over another and propelled me into a journey of truly trusting the child.

As therapeutic parenting became more organic and natural for me, I found myself using the same phrasing in the classroom that I used at home, and saw my own students in my Montessori 3-to 6-year-old classroom respond favorably. Trauma-informed practices married beautifully with Montessori philosophy. More reading and research led to a deeper understanding of the science behind adverse childhood experiences, developmental trauma, neurology, and resilience. I began to see clearly that it was vital for all teachers to assume this new lens through which to see their interactions with students. I began to share what I had learned in small groups, with co-teachers, with like-minded folks I'd met in professional development opportunities, and then by speaking at conferences. When I began to speak out, I found people had two reactions: folks either asked me to come share with their schools and communities, or they said, "I don't serve a population of children who have experienced trauma." There's no faster way to find me on a soapbox than to tell me such a nonsensical hypothesis. Every single population on Earth is affected by childhood trauma, and we often have no way of knowing who in our classrooms may be experiencing trauma. This erroneous assumption on the part of otherwise wonderful educators introduced me to the direct intersection of trauma-informed care and equity work in education. In our adoption groups, I'd often worked with transracial adoptive families as they discovered the unique needs of parenting a child of a different race. Beyond learning to properly care for hair, or speak another language, there were new levels of awareness surfacing for parents as they now understood the realities faced by many people of color. These parents faced microaggressions, racism, and culturally insensitive comments from friends, family members, and yes, even teachers. Teachers and administrators are learning to challenge implicit bias, structural inequity, and support culturally responsive teaching. However, as we are in the process of this shift in school climates across the USA, there are children having adverse childhood experiences in the classroom daily.

Educational trauma is rarely discussed in teacher education programs. Yet ask any group of educators why they became teachers and you will be inundated with a litany of negative school experiences, often deeply disturbing, that led them to education in order to improve the experience for future generations. Educational trauma comes in a variety of forms. While it is sometimes the result of directly inappropriate comments to a student, harsh discipline measures, or bullying, educational trauma is just as often the result of thoughtless expressions of bias in assignments, conversations, or school culture. It has become evident that the most imperative task of trauma-informed care has been to "Do No Harm." This requires lots of internal work on the part of the educator and administrator. It requires "tearing out our most deeply rooted defects" and is often painful and uncomfortable for us (Montessori, 1936/1982, p. 149).

Because I came to trauma-informed practices as a parent, I started this journey of talking to teachers through the lens of an adult serving the needs of children (mine, specifically). I was quickly reminded when talking to teachers that teachers are also humans. Humans have adverse childhood experiences (ACEs), and as adult humans, we aren't always particularly adept at resolving or addressing the reverberations of these experiences. Those experiences are often carried with us into the classroom each day and then influence our own teaching practices in one way or another. Teachers often told me children with difficult-to-manage behavioral challenges called up their own fears of inadequacy, drew attention to the lack of appropriate schoolwide supports that challenged administrators, and frustrated even the deepest believer in positive guidance. Teachers recalled how a student's challenges seemed to directly hit them in their own childhood trauma, and brought them to an impasse of power struggles and school suspensions. The need for teacher self-care underscored their own ability to "Do No Harm." Doing the work of creating healing in our own lives is an evolving practice that includes mental health care, work-life balance, and healthy boundaries.

Though the task is lofty, our classrooms can become places where children, and perhaps teachers too, can learn to build resilience. Beginning in the Infant & Toddler classrooms, we must consider healthy emotional development. For the youngest learner, that means an appropriate response to cries. When infants communicate, we teach them so much about the world by our responses. When we respond quickly and lovingly, we teach them they are safe and that their needs will be met. This is the foundation of the social emotional health they will experience over their lifetime. Babies whose needs and cries are not met learn that they are alone, must survive on their own, and learn a general mistrust for adults. This attachment theory (Bowlby, 1969) is illustrated here.

Attachment Cycle

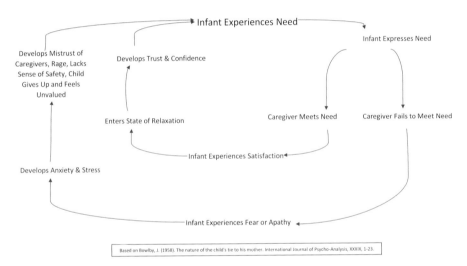

Based on Bowlby, J. (1958). The nature of the child's tie to his mother. International Journal of Psycho-Analysis, XXXIX, 1-23.

As Montessorians, we believe in the importance of the first plane of development. Attachment theory agrees that these first few years of life are vitally important to a child's overall well-being. For the Infant & Toddler environment, the need for the teacher to respond to the child is the most basic, most important care we can provide them. This is especially important for infants who may have experienced prenatal trauma, traumatic birth, or who may not be receiving responsive care at home.

However, the need for responsive care doesn't end in infancy. As children grow, and we continue to observe their development, our classrooms should evolve to reflect their developmental needs. As many children will inevitably experience adverse childhood experiences (ACEs), either with or without our knowledge, it is wise for us to implement trauma-informed practices as a universal precaution. Here are some first steps for creating a trauma-sensitive school.

Creating Felt Safety: We often assume that a child is safe in our classroom without checking to see if the child knows and feels a sense of safety. To ensure students are building resilience and capacity for learning, we can create systems of "Felt Safety." Felt Safety is safety that is explicitly communicated; designed to meet children's physiological, social, and emotional needs; and consistently applied in the classroom and throughout the school. This simple checklist is a beginning activity to ensure you are covering some common needs. You can add to this list as you build a relationship with your students and more fully understand each individual child's needs.

- Snacks (especially those high in protein) and water are available to my students at all times.
- Fidgets, doodling, and sensory items are available to each child in the room.
- The classroom is a calm, uncluttered environment that is not overstimulating.
- Intentional teaching of personal regulation methods is being done and applied on a regular basis.
- There is a place for students to go to find solitude, without repercussions or consequences, and a plan is in place to support the varied needs of multiple students.
- There are known, practiced, and supported classroom procedures in place.
- The routine of the classroom is communicated frequently and is predictable and consistent.
- Children are alerted and supported effectively when changes must occur.
- Supplies are stored in a way that prevents shame for students who may not have the required materials, clothing, jackets, etc.
- Adults who interact with the child are actively seeking the need behind behavior.
- The child is communicated to in a way that ensures a feeling that the teacher is working in collaboration with them, rather than in opposition.
- Adults sit or crouch at children's eye level to speak to them, using a warm gentle tone.
- Teachers aim for twice as many connection-building interactions as corrective actions.
- All adults at the school engage and respect all families and all children.
- The teacher is observant of changes in a child that may indicate they are having a trauma response to events, curriculum, changes, social exchanges, etc.

- Teachers build connected relationships with students that allow them each to bring their most authentic selves to the classroom.

Reaching the Learning Brain: Bruce Perry's work in the field of trauma is an amazing resource for educators. One valuable tool he provides us is the concept of the "3 Rs" of reaching the learning brain (Szalavitz & Perry, 2011).

1. Regulation: When a child is dysregulated and unable to calm down, we must begin by helping them calm the flight/fight/freeze/fawn responses. This could be with co-breathing, providing a hug or sensory item, offering them space and time, a snack, use of an emotional support animal, or using gross motor outlets together. (Self-regulation tools are never punishments and teachers must be wary of allowing the "Peace Corner" to become synonymous with a punitive "time out.")
2. Relate: Connection, Connection, Connection! A child learns best in the context of trusting relationships. We must use this opportunity to create a positive, respectful bond with a child. This attunement to the individual child is a chance to cultivate deep, meaningful interactions during which you gain insight into the child's behavior, emotions, and needs. This tells the child they are still cared for, and never rejected or abandoned, even in moments of undesirable behavior.
3. Reason: With a regulated, reconnected child, we can have reasonable conversations in which true learning can happen. The brain is now able to create new connections, understand cause and effect, and develop new skills. The child can reflect on what has occurred, learn from the situation, and become self-aware.

Author Colleen Wilkinson bonds with her daughter.
Relationship and connection are the most powerful tools to create healing and progress.

Social Coaching & Intentional Teaching: We often see children being reminded to "use your words" when in fact they have little concept of what words to use. They default to words they have discovered have social power, such as, "You aren't invited to my birthday party!" These moments remind us to create intentional teaching about how to communicate frustrations and boundaries respectfully and effectively, as well as teaching children how they can respond when they are hurt by the boundaries set by their peers, how they can negotiate or compromise, and how they can accept the message and move forward. Much of this social coaching happens in the moment as we actively monitor social interactions. Some groups of children may find benefit from role play, group conversations, books, and even some familiar scripted rehearsal. The key concept for teachers to consider is this: "Am I asking my students to have mastered this skill without having first given them a lesson?"

Assessment of Curriculum & Procedures: Often activities in the classroom cause unintentional emotional harm. Activities that ask children to disclose extremely personal information, share childhood photos, create family trees, envision life through the eyes of a colonizing group, or otherwise create situations that can shame, confuse, or cause the child great anxiety, are often sources of educational trauma. Curriculum goals can often be achieved through reframing the activity or lesson. Procedures that are chaotic, cumbersome, have too many steps, or cause sensory overwhelm may challenge children who are struggling to stay regulated. Keeping in mind the child who may be marginalized or harmed, we should evaluate the current procedures and lessons we have in place. If one child is harmed and our classroom is no longer emotionally safe for them, we can expect their behavior and engagement in our class to reflect that new reality. We must adapt to meet the developmental needs of all the children in our class.

Adult Attitudes and Emotions: Children who have experienced trauma are survivors and overcomers. We do them a great disservice if we treat them with pity or assume they need our "saviorism." Our own good boundaries allow us to care deeply for all of our students without creating these unhelpful emotional projections. Instead, we can help them build resilience by believing in all our students' capabilities, creating relationships with them, and seeing behavior as communication. Every single student is worth our effort, and every single teacher must believe it. When we lose our way, we must have a support network of mentors or colleagues, a desire to grow and learn, and a deep personal desire to learn from the children.

The Future of Trauma-Informed Care: Research continues to emerge about the long-lasting impacts of childhood and adult trauma. Epigenetics, the study of heritable phenotype changes, is giving new understanding to intergenerational and historical traumas' impact on the human genome. New techniques for approaching healing have emerged from innovators like Dr. Karyn Purvis, who developed the Trust Based Relational Intervention method, and Dr. Nadine Burke Harris, current California Surgeon General and author of *The Deepest Well*. Currently, the trauma-informed movement is rooted in bringing awareness and understanding to schools and institutions. As we move toward an educational system based on resilience and healing, Montessori schools are uniquely positioned to be forerunners in the well-being of children and our society.

Montessori schools already provide sensory calming classrooms, a commitment to positive child guidance, and a prepared environment and prepared adult(s). Montessori schools all across the world are learning more about trauma-informed discipline, the need for implementation of trauma-informed practices as a universal precaution for every student, and the neuroscience of resilience. With our existing pedagogy and our evolving understanding, Montessorians are capable of helping create a more resilient society for generations to come. Together we can change the world.

CHAPTER 10

Including Young Children with Severe Disabilities in Raintree Montessori School: The Circle of Inclusion

Barbara Thompson and Pamela Shanks

Barbara Thompson holds a PhD in Special Education and served for 30 years as a faculty member in the Early Childhood program area in the Department of Special Education at the University of Kansas. Prior to her work as a teacher educator she was early childhood special education teacher and early childhood program supervisor for 15 years. Barbara is committed to inclusive early childhood education programs that allow young children with and without disabilities to get to know each other and develop positive relationships at this formative period of their lives. As a teacher educator, Barbara's work has been directed at preparing educators to implement learning supports and instructional strategies that facilitate the full membership of young children with significant physical, sensory, intellectual, and health needs in inclusive early childhood classrooms. She believes that Montessori education is uniquely suited to providing high quality and successful inclusive education.

Pam Shanks, MSE, has been involved in both Montessori and special education for her entire teaching career, including over 30 years as the lead guide in an inclusive classroom at Raintree Montessori School. She was involved in several innovative special education projects including the Circle of Inclusion and the Inclusive Network of Kansas. She is AMS-credentialed (Early Childhood). Pam currently serves as the associate head of school at Bowman School in Palo Alto, CA where she continues to support Montessori teachers and inclusive education. She firmly believes that Montessori classrooms are a natural fit for all children no matter their needs or strengths, and she has seen a wide variety of children develop, learn, and thrive together.

At the time our story began, inclusive programs focused almost exclusively on children with mild disabilities. In the eyes of many, their higher level of skill deemed them "appropriate" for an inclusive experience. Children who experienced severe or multiple disabilities, including combinations of mental retardation, deaf-blindness, orthopedic impairments, health impairments, sensory impairments, etc., were considered too disabled to benefit from inclusive programs. These assumptions were negated after a transformative experience in a Primary classroom at Raintree Montessori School in Lawrence, KS served as motivation for the development of a model of inclusion focused on this isolated population of learners. This model, The Circle of Inclusion, began at Raintree with the inclusion of young children with severe multiple disabilities in Primary classrooms. The project demonstrated that children with even the most severe disabling conditions could learn in classrooms alongside peers and that their experiences together held benefits for all. The child at the heart of our story attended Raintree as a result of the co-authors' shared perspective. As we look back, we believe the stars were aligned.

Pam's Story

I found Raintree Montessori School, owned by Keith and Lleanna McReynolds, in 1982, during my undergraduate work in early childhood education at the University of Kansas. At the time, Raintree was a small school that served Primary-age children. Keith and Lleanna were dedicated to Montessori for all children, including those from working families, so they offered both full-day and half-day classrooms. Although I knew little to nothing about Montessori, I was hired to help with early morning care and had the privilege of working with Lleanna, a dedicated master teacher who quickly became a mentor. After graduation, I worked for a year in her classroom as an assistant. I fell in love with the Montessori approach to education, enrolled in Montessori teacher training the following year, and was soon the lead guide in a Raintree Primary classroom.

At Raintree, screening was not a part of the enrollment process by design; open spaces went to the next child on the waiting list. Therefore, from inception Raintree was a welcoming, inclusive school. When a young child in one of my first classes was having trouble learning letter names and sounds, I signed up for coursework in early childhood special education, hoping to find answers.

About the same time, Lleanna asked if I would welcome Claire (all children's names are pseudonyms), a sweet little girl with a severe visual impairment, into my classroom. Mary Gordon, a dedicated teacher of the visually impaired from the local school district, agreed to help me meet Claire's needs. Together, we adapted materials and lessons, long before this kind of collaborative support was established practice. Claire flourished! She learned to count, identify the braille alphabet, prepare and clean up her own snack, and travel independently to the playground and bathroom. Watching her progress was awe-inspiring.

I recognize the importance of all I learned from Mary and Claire. Mary helped me learn to teach academic and mobility skills, and in the process, I gained confidence in individualizing my lessons. The term "prepared environment" took on an entirely new meaning. Practical Life lessons were done slowly. For example, I let Claire explore each part of a pitcher with her hands and then gave the lesson with Claire's hands over mine, so she could *feel what I did* with the pitcher. I also quickly learned I had to talk during her lessons. In my Montessori training, I had been taught to use concise language, but for Claire, a running narrative was the key to education. I adapted my lessons and approach to meet Claire's needs, while simultaneously maintaining the integrity of the same lessons for her friends. In the process, I became a true Montessori guide, a scientist in my own room who considered each child an individual. Motivated to continue special education coursework, I enrolled in more classes, where I would meet the next mentor who would change the course of my career: Barbara Thompson.

Barbara's Story

When I was 14, I began serving as a volunteer in a summer program at a center for children and youth with disabilities—this was in 1957, many years before the passage of federal legislation that mandated education for all children. This program gave me the unique opportunity to develop meaningful friendships with peers who experienced severe disabilities.

I quickly formed a relationship with 12-year-old Emily, who experienced spastic quadriplegia associated with cerebral palsy. Emily's very tight limbs meant she could not walk and had poor head and trunk control. During that summer, we developed a firm friendship grounded in mutual affinity. I still remember her beautiful brown eyes, thick dark hair, and infectious smile. Emily and I talked on the phone, spent time at each other's homes, and took regular trips to a city park near my home. I have many memories of our ventures to the park's small zoo and to the playground area where I somehow managed to lift her from her wheelchair and to hold her tightly as we enjoyed the swings, the merry-go-round, and the slide.

As fall approached, I discovered that some of my summer friends would not be attending the program during the school year. At the time, children and youth with "severe mental retardation" were excluded from public schools. Emily was not eligible, the director explained, because she was "too 'retarded' to benefit." I was stunned and filled with a sense that a profound injustice was occurring.

Emily's family, lacking resources for her education, placed her in a state institution. Later that year, I was devastated to learn that Emily had passed away. I came to view the policies that denied my friends with disabilities access to public school education as profoundly unjust and wrong. I also realized these policies prevented children like Emily and me from developing meaningful relationships. Determined to make a difference, I became a special education teacher and eventually a teacher educator.

While teaching my early childhood special education methods course, I met Pam Shanks. Pam had a reputation for being a gifted teacher at Raintree Montessori School, one of the most respected educational programs in Lawrence, KS. During my graduate studies, I was fascinated with Montessori's early work with children with disabilities and her subsequent contributions to the education of children with disabilities (Gitter, 1967, 1971; Orem, 1969). Her books (c.f. Montessori, 1914/1965, 1949/1967, 1936/1983) led me to appreciate her contributions to child development, educational curriculum, environmental design, and pedagogy. Thus, I viewed Pam's participation in my course as providing me with a significant learning opportunity. Furthermore, Pam was in my class because she was intensely committed to acquiring the knowledge and skills necessary to ensure that children with the full range of disabilities could be successful members of her classroom. I recognized a kindred spirit.

Our Path to Inclusive Education

The following fall, I (Barbara) met Dana in a state residential setting for individuals with developmental disabilities. Dana, a 3-year-old beauty with enormous brown eyes, thick dark hair, olive skin, and a smile that spoke directly to my heart, experienced severe disabilities including a vision disability, an intellectual disability, and spastic quadriplegia. She could not walk, had no vocal speech, limited head control, impacted vision, and could not sit unsupported. When I met Dana, she was lying on a mat in an overcrowded day room, surrounded by people of all ages (mostly adults) with profound disabilities and medically fragile conditions. The only speaking voices came from a large TV bolted to the wall about 8 feet above the floor.

Soon after I met Dana, she was placed in a loving foster home; however, the only special education preschool program available was not serving preschoolers with severe disabilities, as special education services for preschool-aged children were not fully mandated at that time.

I immediately contacted Pam and, after describing Dana, asked if she thought it would be possible to enroll Dana in her classroom at Raintree. I offered to collaborate and provide support via our graduate practicum program. Pam was clearly excited about this possibility and promised to visit with Raintree's administration. Shortly thereafter, Pam called me with her answer: "When would you like her to start?" In Pam's own words,

> Keith and Lleanna opened the door. They welcomed a sweet little girl to Raintree. The fact that 3-year-old Dana did not yet walk or talk was not a consideration any more than the fact that Claire could not see. It was a simple kindness with a profound impact. Their acceptance became mine by example, and because of it, my life changed forever.

Soon after Dana began attending Raintree, I (Barbara) made an initial visit to observe her in Pam's classroom. It actually took me several moments to find her among the children! Her presence in this Children's House was such a marked contrast to my memory of Dana in the institution; seeing her in the classroom was one of the most emotional experiences of my life. Dana was surrounded by happily engaged peers who accepted her as one of them—which of course she was. Pam and I came to understand that my initial encounter with Dana at Raintree was transformational. It was the "aha" moment that confirmed our vision of *all* children as valued and participating members of their schools and communities.

Building Our Vision for All Children

Dana's experience was so successful that we eagerly began work to establish a formal best-practice model program for the inclusion of young children with severe disabilities in both Montessori and traditional Early Childhood classrooms. As one of the research projects within the Kansas Early Childhood Research Institute on Transitions, which was funded from 1988 to 1993 (Rice & O'Brien, 1993), we were able to expand and investigate our work at Raintree. We called our project The Circle of Inclusion.

Our initial focus was directed toward the inclusion of young children with severe multiple disabilities. We emphasized this population based on several factors, including:

- The value of friendships between young children with typical development and those with disabilities (Buysse & Bailey, 1993; Diamond, Hestenes, Carpenter & Innes, 1997; Guralnick, 1990; Hanline, 1993; McLean & Hanline, 1990; Jenkins, Odom, & Speltz, 1989)

- The fallacy of the assumption held by many special education and related service professionals that inclusive placements should go to children with mild disabilities and not to children with severe disabilities (Avramidis & Norwich, 2002; Hanline, 1993; Thompson & Guess, 1989)
- The need for high-quality childcare for young children with severe disabilities (Axtell et al. 1995; Bailey, Blasco & Simeonsson 1992; Booth-LaForce & Kelly 2004; Berk & Berk, 1982).

From 1986 to 1993, 10 young children with severe multiple disabilities were included in Primary classrooms at Raintree. One child with significant disabilities was placed with 23 typically developing peers per Primary classroom to maintain a ratio that most closely matched natural population proportions, as detailed in The Circle of Inclusion values (see Table 2, page 126). These children experienced complex disabilities such as deaf-blindness and cerebral palsy; many had compound medical needs and significant cognitive, language, and motor delays. Table 1 details their ages, diagnoses, and assessed developmental levels at the time of their Raintree enrollment.

Table 1. **Children Participating in The Circle of Inclusion Program at Raintree Montessori School: 1986–1990**

Raintree Entry Date	Age in Months	Gender	Primary Diagnosed Condition(s)	Assessed development in months at entry into inclusive program			
				Cognitive[a]	Social[a]	Language[a]	Motor[a]
10/6/86	39	F	Deaf-blind, Cerebral palsy	0–6	6–18	0	G. 0–6 F. 0–6
2/1/88	41	M	Cerebral palsy, Microcephaly	1–6	8–15	E. 3–8 R. 3–9	G. 2–5 F. 1–4
2/1/88	56	M	Deaf-blind	3–8	6–9	E. 4–6 R. 6–7	G. 5–6 F. 5–9
2/8/89	39	M	Cerebral palsy	3–6	6–7	E. 6–7 R. 10	G. 3–6 F. 3
2/8/89	35	M	Cerebral palsy	6–9	9–15	E. 4–6 R. 8–10	G. 6 F. 3–6
4/3/89	46	M	Down syndrome	22–27	28–30	E. 28 R. 28	G. 24 F. 26

Continued on next page.

Continued from previous page.

Raintree Entry Date	Age in Months	Gender	Primary Diagnosed Condition(s)	Assessed development in months at entry into inclusive program			
				Cognitive[a]	Social[a]	Language[a]	Motor[a]
4/3/89	51	F	Down syndrome	36–48	36–39	E. 34 R. 32–37	G. 26 F. 24
9/28/89	52	F	Cerebral palsy, Visual impairment	11–12	11–18	E. 8–9 R. 8–10	G. 6–15 F. 12–15
9/10/90	60	F	Cerebral palsy, Microcephaly	24–36	24–36	E. 19 R. 36	G. 18–21 F. 6–15
9/10/90	56	F	Down syndrome	30–42	32–34	E. 19 R. 8–30	G. 18–21 F. 28

Notes: [a] Represents the categories of development assessment, i.e., Cognitive, Social, Language (*E.* =*Expressive* & *R.* =*Receptive*) & Motor (*G.* =*Gross* & *F.* =*Fine*) for which the range of sub-scores in months (e.g., 3–6 months or 11–18 months) was obtained for each of the 10 children. The assessments were conducted by special education and related service professionals from the public school district special education program.

Implementation Strategies

Six implementation strategies were critical to the success of The Circle of Inclusion model. To include children with severe and profound disabilities, we focused on the following strategies:

1. Establish a shared value base to guide our work
2. Create a "facilitator" model to support the successful participation of the children
3. Provide training and support for the personnel directly involved with the provision of educational and therapeutic services to the children in their Montessori classrooms
4. Identify and utilize the inherent advantages of Montessori philosophy and materials for inclusive education
5. Employ instructional strategies grounded on a milieu and naturalistic approach
6. Employ strategies that supported friendships among all children

Including Young Children with Severe Disabilities: The Circle of Inclusion

A student with spastic quadriplegia and his good friend
work with matching cards with their teacher, Pam Shanks.

A student with deafblindness works with the Knobbed Cylinders
and puts his rug away, with facilitation from Pam Shanks.

A student with spastic quadriplegia visits with Pam and a typically developing friend.
The typically developing child went on to work at Raintree Montessori School as an adult.

Implementation Strategy 1: Establish a Shared Value Base

The development of collaborative relationships among The Circle of Inclusion stakeholders was essential to the success of the program at Raintree. However, collaboration was challenged by the participation of individuals representing multiple public and private systems, disciplines, and perspectives. Our shared value base, so integral to our story, laid the groundwork for collaborative relationships and offered a way to address potential roadblocks to implementation. Table 2 sets forth the seven values of The Circle of Inclusion project.

Table 2. **Explicit Value Base of The Circle of Inclusion Project**

Value 1: Children should not have to meet criteria to participate in childcare and classroom environments. We reject the notion that children with disabilities must be "fixed" (frequently couched in terms of meeting certain criteria) before they are ready to take their place in families, neighborhoods, and community environments and experience the normal flow of everyday life and friendship available to those without disabilities. Specifically, we believe that preschool children with severe disabilities and their families must have the opportunity for inclusion in high-quality childcare and preschool programs within the mainstream of community programs available to typically developing children and their families.
Value 2: Children with disabilities and children who are typical in their development have the right to get to know each other and develop relationships. We recognize that typically developing preschoolers must have opportunities to develop relationships with children who experience a wide range of disabling conditions. We acknowledge the importance of children learning to live in a pluralistic society and accept individual differences at an early age. We believe that typically developing preschool children are at a critical readiness period for the experience of knowing a child with a disability and that their lives will be enriched by reaching out to friends who experience disabilities.
Value 3: A viable program of full inclusion must reflect collaboration and involvement among all the adult participants. We believe that a viable program must reflect involvement, input, and ongoing collaborative efforts from all participants: the inclusive early childhood program personnel, the special education personnel that provide services and supports to the children in the program, and the families of children in the program.

> *Value 4: The uniqueness and dignity of each child must be valued, preferences acknowledged, choice making supported, and the application of aversive procedures rejected.*
> We hold deep respect for the uniqueness and dignity of each child as an individual human being who merits our careful observation and response to his or her needs. We reject the application of any aversive procedures and believe that the acknowledgment of child preference and the development of choice making skills, a sense of self, and personal autonomy are critical.

> *Value 5: Inclusive programming must incorporate recommended and exemplary practices.*
> We believe that inclusive programing efforts must incorporate best practice approaches that include social interactions with typically developing peers and functional instructional objectives that are taught and practiced using developmentally appropriate activities and materials available to all children in the program. Additionally, a child's individual educational plan (IEP) objectives must be based on family priorities and developed with input from the family and the interdisciplinary team of service providers. The principle of partial participation should be used to maximize involvement when the child is not able to perform all aspects of an activity.

> *Value 6: The concept of natural proportions should guide placement decisions.*
> We accept the concept of natural proportions and believe that it is best to place young children with severe disabilities in "mainstream" programs in accordance with realistic population distributions of individuals with disabilities within the general population.

> *Value 7: Time and energy should be directed toward investigating variables that make inclusive education successful.*
> Our time and energy should be vested in investigating the variables that make inclusive educational endeavors work in the best possible way.

Thompson, B., Wickham, D., Wegner, J., Ault, M., Shanks, P., & Reinertson, B. (1993). Reprinted *from Handbook for the inclusion of young children with severe disabilities: Strategies for implementing exemplary full inclusion programs.* Lawrence, KS: Learner Managed Designs, Inc., pp.19–22).

Implementation Strategy 2: Create a Facilitator Model to Support Successful Child Participation

Raintree's classrooms typically enrolled 20 to 24 children and were staffed by a Montessori guide and a classroom assistant. Because young children with severe disabilities were unable to fully participate in most classroom activities without significant assistance and support, we placed an additional teaching assistant in each inclusive classroom. This allowed the Montessori guides to fully meet the developmental and educational needs of children with significant disabilities, while also ensuring those children's full participation in the social fabric of the classroom community. In keeping with Montessori philosophy and our value base, we decided to call this additional support person a *facilitator* rather than a para-educator or teaching assistant. The facilitator did not "educate" per se, but instead facilitated interactions with materials and others, allowing the child with disabilities to learn from activities and typically developing peers. Facilitators received the same training required of Raintree's classroom assistants, as well as training in the skills and techniques specific to the needs and strengths of the child with a disability assigned to their classroom.

Funding for the facilitators was a significant challenge. The public school district provided Early Childhood special education teachers and related service providers as part of a child's individual education plan at the time that the project was initiated. However, there were no funds to support hiring an additional person (i.e., a facilitator). We addressed this need through funding from grants awarded to the Department of Special Education Early Childhood Special Education Program. Thus, the initial facilitators were primarily graduate Early Childhood special education students who were receiving either grant-based stipends for participation in inclusive field-related experiences or direct funds for employment on the grants.

As the project continued, Early Childhood special education students enrolled in student teaching or fulfilling practicum requirements were placed in the classrooms at Raintree that included a child with significant disabilities. (Such placements at Raintree and in other inclusive Early Childhood settings continue to the present.) Raintree also contributed funds via reduced or fully waived tuition for the initial 10 children and, at times, hired staff. On several occasions, the public school district paid for a facilitator using funds designated for a special education para-educator. After Pam earned dual special education teaching licenses in Early Childhood Special Education and Severe Multiple Disabilities and could serve as an Early Childhood special educator, the school district reimbursed Raintree for 1/10th of her salary. These funds were used to offset some of the costs associated with The Circle of Inclusion project.

Implementation Strategy 3: Educate and Support the Direct Service Personnel

Each child arrived at Raintree with instructional and therapeutic goals identified in an Individualized Education Program (IEP). Thus, each child had a special educator and, depending on identified needs, related service personnel (i.e., physical therapist, occupational therapist, speech-language therapist and/or a school nurse) from the local public school district who were assigned to support implementation of a child's IEP goals and benchmarks. It is important to note that with the establishment of The Circle of Inclusion Project, once a child was placed at Raintree, the lead Montessori educator for the classroom in which the child was placed became a member of the child's IEP team.

The Montessori classroom educator, Montessori classroom assistant, facilitator, and the public school special education and related service personnel formed what we now think of as an educational team. We came to recognize that the adults involved had the power to affect our program's success or failure. Differences in beliefs and implementation of educational methodology between the special education personnel and the Montessori educators were immediately apparent, as was the need to educate and support these adults (Horn, Thompson, Nelson, 2004; Klein & Sheehan, 1987; Thompson et. al, 1993).

Many of the Early Childhood special education teachers and therapeutic personnel had concerns about the well-being of children with significant disabilities in a non-specialized setting. They felt unsure about effectively implementing their specialized roles in an inclusive setting. Additionally, most were unfamiliar with Montessori methodology and materials.

The Montessori educators sometimes viewed the special education methods and approaches as intrusive or contrary to their philosophy. While the guides and assistants at Raintree were enthusiastic about participating, they were also unsure about their ability to properly handle a child with significant and complex physical disabilities and/or special health care needs. It was critical to ensure that the Montessori guide, classroom assistant, and facilitator were equally comfortable facilitating, handling, interacting with, and caring for these children.

With support and training, skills and perspectives evolved. Raintree's staff gained confidence and became skillful in handling, interacting with, and instructing the children with significant disabilities. The special education program personnel became much more positive and supportive of inclusive practices and were able to function comfortably and appropriately in Montessori classrooms. Most importantly, the lead Montessori teacher was truly the lead teacher for *all* of the children, including the child with a disability. The facilitator supported the child with disabilities as needed when the Montessori staff were working with other children. Special education and related service personnel respectfully delivered services in classrooms which allowed facilitators, Montessori educators, and at times, peers, to learn some of the therapeutic techniques of benefit to the children with disabilities. When a therapist arrived to work with a child, facilitators and/or the Montessori teachers could observe to improve their understanding and skills. Facilitators were also free to step back and observe the classroom as a whole to further their understanding of Montessori philosophy and materials. Thus, each classroom functioned as a traditional Montessori classroom.

The children formed close, beneficial relationships with their friends with disabilities quickly. While it took time and understanding for the adults, they too formed respectful, mutually beneficial educational teams. In the broadest sense of the word, we all learned from each other.

Implementation Strategy 4: Recognize and Utilize the Inherent Advantages of Montessori Educational Materials and Methods for Inclusive Education

Dr. Montessori developed her philosophy of education around a core set of observations, values, and practices rooted in her early work with children with disabilities (Gitter, 1971; Orem, 1969). Lena Gitter (1971) cited Montessori as the first professional to make the important leap from regarding retardation (as she called it) as a medical issue to thinking of it as a joint medical and educational problem.

Throughout our work, we identified many features of the Montessori method of education that are especially conducive to successful inclusive experiences for young children with severe to profound disabilities (Gitter, 1967; Shanks, 1990; Shanks, 2009; Thompson et al. 1991; Thompson et al., 1993). The critical nature of sensory activities and materials during the early childhood period for children who experience the many sensory delays common to a diagnosis of severe and profound disabilities were also apparent (Dunn, 1997; Horn and Kang, 2012; Shanks, 2009) and established the value of the unique and well-designed sensorial materials found in Montessori classrooms. Table 3 sets forth these features and includes aspects of the philosophy, the prepared environment, and the didactic materials.

Table 3. **The Right Match: Features of the Montessori Method That Support Inclusive Education for Young Children with Severe Disabilities**

Feature 1: Emphasis on Community
A Montessori Primary classroom is an interconnected community of learners of mixed ages naturally providing opportunities for meaningful and supportive relationships. The 3-year age span creates a broad diversity of development, so, as in families, older children naturally help, mentor, teach, and care for those who are younger or less able.
Feature 2: Individualized Approach
Montessori materials provide a broad range of instructional opportunities allowing children, both with and without disabilities, to work to their individual strengths and needs.
Feature 3: Sensorial Materials
The sequence of Sensorial materials in Montessori Primary classrooms holds advantages for children who experience a broad range of sensory impairments or processing disorders that often occur in combination with intellectual disorders and physical disabilities.
Feature 4: Practical Life
This area, unique to the Montessori method, benefits children who experience disabilities by offering opportunities to develop life skills in natural, meaningful contexts and routines.
Feature 5: Montessori Lessons
Naturally designed to be precise, orderly, and consistent, Montessori lessons are delivered using concise language, emphasizing a logical progression from the beginning of a task to its end. Thus, Montessori lessons share important qualities with instructional techniques from the field of special education.
Feature 6: Repetition
The Montessori method values repetition, and learners with disabilities often require repeated practice to master a skill.

Table 4 offers examples of how one Montessori material, the Sound Cylinders, was used to meet individual educational objectives common among children with severe disabilities. In all examples provided, peers could and did perform the role of the facilitator with careful training and support. Once a routine was established and both children were comfortable, adults stepped back to observe. As you read these examples in Table 4, imagine two children, one with disabilities and one with typical development, performing the actions.

Table 4. **Using Montessori Materials to Meet Individual Education Plan (IEP) Goals and Objectives Common to Young Children Experiencing Severe to Profound Disabilities: Examples Using the Sound Cylinders**

- **Auditory Awareness, Attention, and Localization of Sound:**
    - Awareness: Look for and encourage any response on the part of the child to the sounds of the cylinders, including a change in facial expression or posture
    - Attention: Reinforce increasing lengths of awareness to sound
    - Localization: Move the cylinder to the left or right of the child and reinforce orienting, head turn or other directional attention
- **Visual Attending and Tracking:**
    - Visual attention: Guide the student to look at the cylinder and shake it* or allow the student to shake it as a natural consequence for looking
    - Tracking: Encourage the child to follow the cylinder horizontally or vertically across the visual field

    *Note: The noises made by the cylinders may naturally draw and reinforce the visual attention of the child
- **Reach, Grasp and Release:**
    - Reach: Guide the child to reach and touch a cylinder to make a sound
    - Grasp: Hold and shake the cylinder
    - Release: Hand the cylinder to friend, practicing release
- **Communication:**
    - Vocal or non-verbal communication: Ask the child questions and encourage a vocalization or sign to indicate:
        - "more" for another turn
        - "yes" to indicate that a friend should shake the cylinders again
- **Head Control and Strength:**
    - Head control: Encourage the child to hold up her head before shaking the cylinders
    - Head turn: Shake to the left or right side to encourage head movement
- **Turn Taking:**
    - Children take turns using the cylinders, thus reinforcing the reciprocal nature of social interaction

Implementation Strategy 5: Employ Instructional Strategies Grounded on a Milieu and/or Naturalistic Approach

We firmly believed that all children should feel like an accepted member of a group and experience the joy that comes from true involvement and accomplishment. Hence, the instructional strategies we employed to meet the needs of children with significant disabilities embedded instruction and therapeutic services into the existing activities and routines of their Raintree classroom. This approach is identified in the literature as a milieu approach and/or naturalistic approach (c.f. Grisham-Brown & Hemmeter, 2017; Horn, Palmer, Butera, & Lieber, 2016; Horn, Thompson, Palmer, & Jenson, & Turbiville, 2004; Noonan & McCormick, 2014; Sandall & Schwartz, 2008; Thompson et al., 1996).

Sharing this perspective, we identified and used three overarching inclusive strategies to support the instructional experiences of the children with disabilities. These included: (A) using child-initiated activities to guide instructional experiences by acknowledging the child's preferences and offering appropriate choices available in their Montessori classroom; (B) encouraging cooperative and helpful interactions with peers by employing the principle of partial participation on the part of the child with a disability; and (C) embedding the child's IEP objectives within the Montessori routines and activities in meaningful and functional ways.

A. **Acknowledge preferences and support choice making.** Commonly, adults do too much for children with severe disabilities, thereby limiting the development of a sense of autonomy. This is particularly problematic when children cannot express their preferences and/or move without assistance (Cannella, O'Reilly, & Lancioni, 2005).

Offering meaningful choices to children with severe disabilities is particularly suited to Montessori classrooms, as the philosophy supports individuality and choice. For Raintree students, this required an understanding of the child's nonverbal communication and cues and was based on sensitive child observation, a hallmark of the Montessori guide. Choice making was a natural fit.

For example: *Jacob uses his eye gaze and looks in the direction or area of the room where he wants to move, looks at the material he wants to use, or indicates he would enjoy having a child join him by an affirmative head nod.* (Thompson et al., 1993, pp. 167–168)

B. **Encourage cooperative and helpful interactions with peers that employ the principle of partial participation.** In many instances, children with severe disabilities can meaningfully participate in an activity even if they are unable to do all steps of the activity. The principle of partial participation advocates for providing individuals with disabilities the opportunity to use a material and/or be a part of an activity by identifying the part or parts they *can do* (Baumgart et al., 1982). We implemented this principle by (a) adapting materials and activities and (b) by having an adult or a typically developing peer(s) do the part(s) the child with a disability could not. We considered it essential that *all* of the children (i.e., both children with disabilities and children with typical development) who participated in an activity do so in a way that was both enjoyable and beneficial to their development.

For example: *Lisa is able to match the correct picture with an object. She indicates her selection by gazing at the object (a goal on her IEP), but she is unable to actually place the object on the card. She and Shelley, her classmate and friend, can take turns selecting the correct object, while Shelley physically places all the objects on the cards. In this way, both children participate in a valuable and enjoyable learning activity. Lisa participates in an activity that would not be possible for her under the usual circumstances, while Shelley, her typically developing partner, has the added benefit of helping a friend.* (Thompson et al., 1993, p. 169)

C. **Embed individual child objectives in the Montessori classroom routines and activities in meaningful ways.** Planning separate activities for a child with a disability compounds the task of educational and related service personnel and works against the tenets of inclusion, immediately and unnaturally setting the included child apart from peers. Young children with disabilities must be involved in the same activities and use the same materials as their peers. This began to happen as the Montessori guide, classroom assistant, and facilitator collaborated with the special education personnel. Eventually, guides, classroom assistants, facilitators, and the special education and related service personnel became adept at making the needed adaptations to ensure the use of Montessori materials and activities to meet IEP objectives.

For example: *Shannon enjoys wiping up her own spills with a sponge and scrubbing the table after snack. She is involved in the natural consequence of cleaning up, which fosters an understanding of personal responsibility and natural consequences within the context of a meaningful application, just as it does for her typical peers.* (Thompson et al., 1993, p. 170).

Shannon, who understands spoken language, but is nonverbal and experiences cerebral palsy and health issues, is learning the sequence of where and how to retrieve the necessary materials needed to wipe the table, as well as how to return them to the proper place when the task is completed. Critical to her objectives, she is standing unsupported at the table, crossing the midline as she wipes the table, and improving her grasp.

Implementation Strategy 6: Employing Strategies that Support Friendships Among the Children

Pam recalls:

> One day, after failing to hold Dana's attention in a lesson, I gave the same lesson to another child who was observing. As I presented, I realized that Dana was watching intently. Not surprisingly, the children were much more interesting to her than I ever could be! So, from that point on, the children worked with Dana as much as possible. Dana was teaching them, and they were teaching her. I watched inclusive experiences shape the lives of children with and without disabilities, and we began to document the range of benefits for both groups.

For a child who is nonverbal, has difficulty understanding oral language, and/or experiences significant physical disabilities, the opportunities for participation in activities with other children are often limited. Someone must identify or create opportunities for interactions and then assist the typically developing children to interpret their peer's nonverbal means of communicating. Adults must mediate initial peer interactions, offering support as the children learn interactive skills and become sensitive to communicative attempts. This process promotes natural, sustained interactions between children rather than adult supported and driven interactions.

In her seminal article on preschool democracy, Susan Krogh (1981, p. 45) pointed out that a Montessori classroom is intended to be an "embryonic, just community" in which children of differing ages and abilities form a sense of community and develop concern and sympathy for the needs of its members. Friendships among children develop because of the positive reciprocal interactions that often occur when a child approaches another child or group of children engaged in activity of interest, and they discuss common interests. Krogh (1982) expanded her discussion of the embryonic society by addressing the potential of the Montessori classroom as a positive environment for the inclusion of young children with disabilities.

Over the course of The Circle of Inclusion project at Raintree, we investigated the strategies and variables that led to sustained friendships between the typically developing children and their peers with severe disabilities. The importance of the role of the adult partner in the development and maintenance of such interactions was confirmed by a number of studies conducted at Raintree (Brooke, 1992; Leon, 1992; Lit, 1993; Kimura, 1991; Stargardter, 1988; Stegemann, 1993; Wegner, 1991). Table 5 lists the six overarching strategies for facilitating communication and social interactions between children with typical development and their peers with severe disabilities, along with specific tactics that support each strategy (Thompson & Wegner, 1992; Thompson et al., 1993).

Table 5. **Six Strategies for Facilitating Social Interaction and Communication Between Children with Typical Development and Their Peers with Severe Disabilities**

Strategy One: Invite and Encourage Participation with Their Classmate with a Disability

- Use a warm and accepting manner with children
- Encourage frequent brief interactions
- Invite children to become involved in an ongoing activity
- Suggest that a child select an activity that will include their classmate
- Facilitate meaningful participation in a natural and helpful manner

Matt and I were sitting and watching a child hold the bowl and work at bubble beating. When another child began his turn, I said, "I'll bet Matt would like to hold the bowl for you; he can be your helper." The child said he didn't need help, but I suggested that Matt was his friend, and friends help each other. Well, I didn't know if that sunk in or not. But then a month later, when I was doing a matching activity with Matt, one of the little girls who had been watching came over and said Matt could be her helper. (Thompson et al., 1993, pp. 148–149)

Strategy Two: Answer Children's Questions About a Classmate with a Disability

- Answer honestly and straightforwardly, in a manner a young child can understand
- Contribute to understanding of disabling conditions and acceptance of the child with a disability
- Convey respect for the child with a disability

One of the children asks, "Why doesn't he say it with words? Pam answers, "Jacob can't talk because his muscles don't work very well, but he knows all about the Sound Cylinders. He can't shake them . . . he nods his head if they are the same. He knows all about them." (Cited from videotape: *The process of communication: Facilitating interactions with young children with severe disabilities in mainstream early childhood programs* (Thompson & Wegner, 1992).

Strategy Three: Offer Meaningful Content on Behalf of the Child with a Disability

- Address ongoing conversations or activities of the children
- Emphasize the similarities among the children
- Relate information as well as experiences, thoughts, and feelings of the child with disabilities

Samantha was crying and a little boy asked me why. I said, "Well, why do you cry? I think she's like you. She probably cries because she gets mad. But she can't tell us why like you can." I was trying to get him to think about Sam's feelings and more about his own feelings, too. This little boy was very shy and quiet, so I think he understood about another child not talking very well. (Thompson et al., 1993, pp. 155–156)

Strategy Four: Teach Children to Interact Directly with Their Classmate with a Disability

- Teach children to recognize and interpret the nonverbal response of their classmate
- Remind children to direct their comments and questions directly to their classmate, rather than to a nearby adult
- Help children include their classmate with a disability in decision-making and choosing activities

Bobby asked me, "Can I work with Jacob?" And I said, "Well, it's okay with me, but go and ask Jacob." So he asked Jacob and was really good about getting down to his eye level and saying, "Jacob, can I do this work with you?" He started to go get the materials, and I asked, "Did you talk about what you were going to do? Why don't you talk about what you're going to do first?" (Thompson et al., 1993, p. 159)

Strategy Five: Allow Spontaneous Interactions to Occur

- Provide assistance without directly participating in interactions (such as remaining close to unobtrusively offer assistance when needed or helping the child with physical movements, like reach and grasp, without interacting with the peer)
- Fade physically from the children's interactions at appropriate times

I was watching Samantha sitting at a table with another little girl. She likes to hold the puzzle pieces and hand them to her friend. I just let her do it on her own. I didn't go across the room, but I stepped away from the table, so it was just the two of them—both happy and very much a part of the class. (Thompson et al., 1993, p. 160)

Strategy Six: Utilize Positioning and Handling to Facilitate Interactions
- Keep child on the same level as peers
- Facilitate movement with materials and peers

We are trying to keep Jacob on the same level with peers whenever possible by having him use/sit in a tumble form floor chair or wedge on the floor (i.e., lie in a supported manner). (Thompson et al., 1993, pp. 162). (Note: these two strategies made it possible for Jacob to do work on the floor with his peers.)

Even though Bruce knows how to do an activity, he sometimes needs help to physically do it. For example, sometimes he can't both interact and concentrate on grasping, so a peer or I will put our hand on top of his to help him through an activity. (Thompson et al., 1993, pp. 161–162).

Lisa was 5 years old when she began attending Raintree. She was unable to sit unsupported, did not speak, and was assessed with a severe intellectual disability. Shortly after Lisa's arrival, her new friend (and typically developing child) Meredith insisted that Lisa wanted to use the bathroom like she did. Her Montessori teacher and occupational therapist came up with a way for Lisa to communicate her need to use the bathroom, and Lisa's participation in the classroom began to change.

> Lisa now wears a bracelet with a touch-sensitive switch. When she needs to use the bathroom, she moves her arm so that the switch is activated, and the soft melodic sounds of a music box play. What a wonderful way for this sweet 5-year-old to discreetly indicate that she needs to be assisted to the bathroom. In the bathroom, Lisa uses an adapted chair with special head and trunk support. Soft vinyl straps hold her securely in the chair, and she no longer has to wear a diaper. Last week, she began using an augmentative communication device with a voice. A 5-year-old girl in another Raintree classroom acted as her new voice, which was recorded on the device. When Lisa wears her hand splint, she can activate her communication board and actually tell her friends hi! We are beginning to find out how many things Lisa knows. She has surprised us all—except, of course, her friend Meredith!

> Lisa knows numbers, letters, colors, and shapes, and recognizes her name in print. She has a new walker that provides almost total support for her trunk. Her teacher said that the first time she tried it out on the playground, she joined a game of tag and laughed with pure joy! (Thompson et al., 1993, p. 129)

The Stars Aligned: Final Reflections

As we moved forward together on the path laid during our work on The Circle of Inclusion project at Raintree, we came to understand that the absorbent nature of the young child's mind assured that children accepted the presence of friends like Dana, Lisa, and Jacob naturally and immediately. They asked questions to better understand what they were seeing and experiencing. However, they never questioned the reason nor the right of any child with a disability to be in their classroom. They never doubted any child's value as a human being. As we witnessed the participation of the children who experienced disabilities and the development of their friendships with their typically developing peers, we were reminded of Dr. Montessori's understanding of the nature of joy:

> Joy, feeling one's own value, being appreciated and loved by others, feeling useful and capable of production are all factors of enormous value for the human soul. (Montessori, 1948/1973).

While inclusion thrives on support and collaboration, it requires an alignment of the values and beliefs that brought us together originally. In the end, we think the most important lesson is that we believed in the same shining star. It is about the children—*all children*. Isn't that really what Montessori is all about?

CHAPTER 11

Elizabeth Academy: Awakening to a New Dawn

Gail Williamsen with Lizzie Dalton and Mandy Fuhriman

Gail Williamsen is executive director and founder of Elizabeth Academy. She is AMS-credentialed (Administrator), and the mother of seven children. Her youngest child, Lauren Elizabeth, has Down syndrome, and was the inspiration for Elizabeth Academy. Gail believes Montessori is an essential element of inclusion. "Inclusion means everyone. Montessori is the best basis for inclusion, as it already addresses individualized learning/lessons, multi-age grouping for a sense of community, following scientifically proven planes of development with material and lessons that target academic goals in a multi-sensorial way. Its greatest hallmark for inclusion's sake, though, is its adaptability, allowing for innovation through the ages of time."

Lizzie Dalton has bachelor's and master's degrees in special education. She holds Montessori credentials for both Early Childhood and Lower Elementary levels. Lizzie joined the Elizabeth Academy staff in 2006 and has been involved in special education for over 10 years through service, teaching in inclusive elementary schools, and providing private services for families with children with special needs. Lizzie's passion is inclusion, and she is dedicated to providing support to the inclusive environment at Elizabeth Academy.

Mandy Fuhriman has a master's degree in special education and a bachelor's degree in therapeutic recreation. She is AMS-credentialed (Early Childhood). Mandy is the inclusion director at Elizabeth Academy and Garfield School. Prior to joining Elizabeth Academy in 2012, Mandy worked as a special educator and an adaptive physical education instructor for the public school systems in both Utah and Arizona. She believes that all students belong and that we need to work together to innovate and create settings where all students are valued and included.

Awakenings

An awakening is like a little light that pierces through darkness. For me, this illumination began with the birth of my seventh child. Lauren Elizabeth Williamsen was born on October 17, 2003 and brought with her a tiny gift. An extra chromosome. The name Lauren means "celestial," which describes her spiritual qualities. The name Elizabeth was chosen to command the earthly respect we felt she would need. Our school thrives on the light she and others like her bring to us. We chose her middle name for our school as we strive to live up to high ideals in education.

Elizabeth Academy began with a tiny awakening and has turned into a model school for inclusive Montessori education. Inclusive education isn't just a career for me. It isn't just theory. I can never put it aside and choose another door. I live inclusion. Every day I manage a school and a family with diverse abilities and needs. Finding a better way for all of these people to be educated, to socialize, and to live, love, and be happy is a daily challenge and a joy to me.

Because I am aware of a desperate and pervasive human need, I feel a personal sense of duty and am tethered to the task. I cannot *not* do it. I admire teachers and administrators greatly for whom education, especially special education, is a freely chosen profession (my colleagues, Lizzie Dalton and Mandy Fuhriman who contribute to this chapter, are two of the most genuinely empathetic people I know). I am grateful for these fine women and the entire community at Elizabeth Academy for constantly striving to meet the ever-changing needs of our school as we develop new programs and strategies to lighten and light the way for others.

We believe that Montessori naturally aligns with numerous best practices of inclusion. Elizabeth Academy is our learning playground, and we invite you to join in our sandbox as we share lessons we have learned along the way.

Discovering Montessori

In October 2006, Lauren turned 3 and became eligible for a special inclusive preschool in Salt Lake City, where we lived. The local school district received special education funding for a few children like her, and filled the rest of the preschool class with mostly "typical" children who paid a very modest price for tuition. To the parents of these "typical" children, it was a convenient and affordable preschool option, but to me it was my only hope for early intervention and a "normal" educational experience for Lauren. ("Typical" has become the word we use in referring to children who don't have disabilities.) I hoped that this school would be the gateway for an education that might give my child the world and a normal life like other "typical" children. But, alas, although the preschool turned out to be a sweet little introduction to school, the early intervention aspects were sorely lacking.

Signing personal checks with a sigh, I supplemented Lauren's learning with private speech therapy and started researching educational alternatives. In 2007, a trusted friend recommended Montessori. With nowhere else to turn, and nothing left to lose, I looked into it. The method made perfect sense, especially when I recognized that *all children* go through a process of "normalization." That word resonated with me instantly.

A local Montessori school cautiously agreed to a 3-week trial for Lauren, and during the trial period, I acted as Lauren's personal aide. One magical day, I heard my little 3-year-old with Down syndrome, who had a vocabulary of barely 10 words at the time (mostly one-syllable utterances), mimic the sounds and words she heard the older children making on the other side of the room, all while she was engaged in a Practical Life activity. Singing to herself, she said, "monkey, monkey, /m/, /m/, /m/."

Monkey! My Lauren just said "monkey" while blissfully scooping beans into a bowl! No teacher or speech therapist hammering that one home. Just the genius of the Montessori method and the spirit of true inclusion. I was hooked.

Lauren Elizabeth Willamsen, age three, with her sister Emma.

Lauren had heard the word "monkey" and its initial sound, /m/, and was compelled to imitate. She exercised her speech musculature and began acquiring new language based on her exposure to language in the environment. I was beginning to truly appreciate the benefit and wisdom of Montessori's multi-age classrooms and the spontaneous peer mentoring that naturally supports and promotes inclusion. Expose children to sounds and words, expose children to the richness of friends in a social setting and all of the wonderful things in the world. As Montessori said (1914/2005, p. 26):

> The children learn from each other and throw themselves into the work with enthusiasm and delight. This atmosphere of quiet activity develops a fellow-feeling, an attitude of mutual aid and, most wonderful of all, an intelligent interest on the part of the older children in the progress of their little companions.

But then, when the 3 weeks were up, Lauren was rejected. I felt such bitterness as I read the dismissal letter. But softly, slowly, the bitter sweetened and my heart turned to a quiet resolve. When I picked up Lauren on her last day, I met her teacher in the empty hall. It was a somber and awkward moment until I sensed another presence awaken my mind and heart to the task at hand. I looked into the apologetic eyes of the kind Montessori teacher who had graciously allowed my child into her classroom and said, "On behalf of countless children who I do not know, I want to thank you for these 3 weeks and for dismissing Lauren. The door that has closed on her today will open a new door for all of tomorrow's children."

With what little knowledge of Montessori I had gained as Lauren's aide in the 3-week trial, and buoyed by faith and conviction, I determined that I would start my own *inclusive* Montessori school. Lauren was the catalyst for this endeavor. But she would not be the only beneficiary.

Team Lauren and the District Preschool

After Lauren's rejection from the Montessori school, she went back to the district preschool. I knew she needed extra support from special education and therapy experts, and I desperately desired the benefits of a Montessori education, so I patched these services together for her first preschool year while hatching a plan for subsequent years to come. Montessori-trained teachers were scarce where we lived, so I decided to find a program to train my own. I gathered together two special educators and sent them to training. For cohesion, I also gifted that training to the teacher from the district preschool who would be Lauren's teacher the following year. Together with Lauren's wonderful private speech therapist, these women comprised my own "Team Lauren." Lizzie Dalton was one of the special educators on the initial team. She recalls the spiritual transformation that took place in the Montessori training she took that summer with the other two women. All three, even the novice district preschool teacher, were thrilled with the Montessori principles they learned, the warmth and congeniality they felt as a team, and the excitement they had to start working together. Then the school year began. Lizzie describes the experience:

When I was in Lauren's classroom, I was asked to sit right next to the children with special needs so they would not "disrupt" too much. The teachers were willing to have us there and this was a step, but it was clear that this was the district's classroom.

Before Team Lauren's first IEP meeting, being extremely naive, I emailed my thoughts to those who would attend the meeting and I included questions about the early intervention aspect of the program. I saw the school as a fairly typical program, without much intervention for a child like Lauren. I thought we might offer the support of Team Lauren to problem-solve those issues together. However, I never expected this meeting would be so emotional.

During the IEP meeting, we sat with six other people from the district. We discussed my email, and our district colleagues expressed how they felt we were questioning their expertise and their methods. The tears started to flow. Gail was willing to pay for Montessori training and for speech therapists and special educators for the classroom, but it felt like a threat to some people.

There was blame, anger and the meeting ended with many people crying. I can remember walking out of the meeting thinking, "What just happened?"

After this meeting, we had to go back into the classroom and piece together the dream of working to create an inclusive Montessori preschool with the district partnership.

One of my greatest blessings has been embarking upon this journey with Lizzie Dalton. She has weathered multiple storms with me. As she describes above, we had many awkward and uncomfortable moments that year when the district personnel and "Team Lauren" clashed. I don't think they appreciated having extra teachers and Montessori strategies imposed upon them. Excitement for innovation is contagious, and inclusion is often uncharted territory. However, mindsets, attitudes, beliefs, and buy-ins are essential. This was missing in our partnership with the district school. We had envisioned a partnership with the district, but when that didn't work, we decided we needed to chart our own course.

However, when Montessorians, special educators and therapists *do* join together in a spirit of collaboration, learning from each other, loving each child and seeing "the child" in every individual (including each adult involved in the process), education rises to a level that exceeds our greatest expectations. This was our first lesson learned, and our happy experience ever since. Still, it is also essential to have a *shared mission, vision,* and *values.*

A School is Born (Myrtle Avenue, 2009–2012)

Elizabeth Academy founder Gail Willamsen, with daughter Lauren and classmates.

By this point, Lauren had missed 2 years of the 3-year Montessori Early Childhood cycle. I was determined to give her Montessori for the third year. So, in 2009, we took the great leap and opened our own school. Elizabeth Academy was born.

Excitement was bubbling, Montessori teachers were trained, and our beautiful classrooms were built out in a former medical office building. But with only 2 weeks before the school was scheduled to start, we had no students (except Lauren) enrolled in the program! We consulted a marketing specialist and landed a spot on the local news (KSL TV, 2013).

Gail Williamsen being interviewed on KSL5.

Enrollment took off and we had 55 students by the time school began. Our first year, we had two Early Childhood classrooms plus another classroom for children with more significant delays. Looking back on the news story from 10 years ago, I am impressed with our optimism and commitment. I still smile at my words in the interview: "I would love to become obsolete." I laugh at my naiveté in thinking that we could change the world of inclusive education in just a few years and I could go back to becoming a normal stay-at-home mom. Many years, many moms, and many other experts later we are still working on it! These and more will always be needed to move the work of inclusive education forward until it becomes part of the infrastructure of an educational norm. And we will never rest. Passionate parents, innovative minds, methods, and the heart of Montessori will move us ever forward. No one in this challenging and dynamic enterprise will ever become "obsolete."

At Elizabeth Academy, our mission statement binds our beliefs and aspirations. The summer before Elizabeth Academy opened, I felt the following words burning in my heart while I was pondering our path. I scribbled them on a scrap of paper and consider them sacred. They have remained unchanged. They embody our deepest shared beliefs and guide us in our mutual quest:

> We believe that on the child rests the future of humanity.
>
> So we must love, value and respect the children, and every child.
>
> All children are unique and we will diligently strive to meet them at their individual need, realizing that this benefits the whole. We will focus on all strengths, overcome weakness, and imagine possibility.

That first year, we were charmed. We had little in the way of experience; nonetheless, the children thrived. Indeed, they lit the way by exemplifying unconditional love and friendship, accepting each other without reservation and embracing their world with wide-eyed wonder. We seemed to have found perfect inclusion. Then we started our second year. We added a Lower Elementary classroom and enrolled older children without Montessori experience to fill the class. Then we unleashed them all on a few overwhelmed and underprepared teachers who had traditional teaching backgrounds, but barely any Montessori or special education experience. We were no longer charmed.

Incredibly, the children in the classroom still thrived, but insecurity took its toll on the teachers and administration. One week before the December holiday program, our newly appointed head-of-school resigned via a group email, clearing out her desk early that morning before anyone else arrived. The lead Elementary teacher, who felt aligned with the head of school, was terribly shaken but gratefully stayed on through the next year.

One thing we have learned as we have grown as a school is that it helps to remember human goodness in any confrontation. We were all good people, with good values; we just did not share a common mission and vision for the school. By the end of Elizabeth Academy's third year, the course we needed to take became abundantly clear. We had to let certain teachers and administrators go. Nevertheless, it had to be done with kindness and the loving truth. We held a luncheon, which served as an end-of-year goodbye and tribute to all our teachers and staff. This one was particularly special. We gave heartfelt thank-you notes to each person, acknowledging them for their service. As we would do in the classroom, we included everyone—those who were leaving, those who were staying, those we loved more, those we loved a little less (after all, we are only human). It changed us. We were as open, honest, and loving as we could be. We all stumble along the way; however, teachers, staff, and administrators must share the same passion and belief in human potential.

Founder Gail Williamsen contemplates the future of Elizabeth Academy.

A Neighborhood School (Connor Street, 2013–2019)

Fortunately, a few great leaders joined our ranks. As we began our fourth year in the fall of 2012, Mandy Fuhriman came on board as an outstanding special educator, and Jennifer Spikner joined us as an experienced, Montessori-trained Elementary teacher. These two women developed and fortified the program from within and then went on to become powerful leaders in our administration. When Jennifer became our head of school, she was a godsend in strengthening our Montessori elements. And when Mandy moved to become director of inclusion, she elevated inclusive structures in ways that had never been done before.

Leadership, common values, and collaboration are not the only essentials in building a successful inclusive school. In 2012, with an Upper Elementary program on the horizon, we decided to build a new facility. The architecture and design took into account elements of inclusion and Montessori philosophy. We moved into this new, modern facility in the fall of 2013. It is a joyful working environment for students and staff alike.

The new state-of-the-art facility benefits the children as well as the teachers.

Along with educational expertise in program operations, organizational structures, and curricular adaptations, there needs to be synergy between the Montessori program and other therapy services. And until inclusion proves itself to be desirable for the typical student, there needs to be a "hook." For us, Montessori was the hook to attract typical children, especially at the Early Childhood level. We needed more hooks as children grew older. It was during this period of developing inclusive practice at the Elementary level that we learned how to utilize therapy services in the classroom as a natural extension of Montessori inclusion. This took the whole program to another level in a number of ways.

In the beginning, our classroom teaching model was comprised of two teachers (a Montessori lead and a special educator) and an assistant for support. Merging Montessori and special education practices could be difficult at times, but usually the two philosophies complemented each other.

In the years between 2013 and 2017, we experimented with a new teaching team model, combining a Montessori lead teacher with a speech-language pathologist (SLP) instead of a special educator. We felt there was a greater need for strong focus on language development. We also combined therapy services of all kinds, both in-class and private, according to each individual child's need. We added weekly in-class support from a music therapist, an occupational therapist, and a physical therapist.

As teachers and therapists were able to meet the needs of all students in the classroom, students' growth improved significantly. Teachers and therapists were also learning from and supporting each other. The collaboration became contagious.

Mandy recalls a difficult first encounter and how it was eventually resolved through collaboration:

> One of the first days that the Toddler Montessori teacher and the SLP teacher began working together in the classroom, the SLP teacher asked a nonverbal child to "use his words" to ask permission to use a particular work. This violated Montessori's philosophical tenets of choice and independence, and the Montessori teacher was appalled. However, the Montessori teacher waited until she could be alone with her SLP co-teacher to discuss the approach. Once the two were able to communicate and collaborate, they agreed that the priority for this particular child was speech. He needed vocabulary, words, and language as prerequisites for his further development in the classroom. Motivating him to "use his words" (discreetly, of course, so he wouldn't be embarrassed by his peers) was "following the child" and giving him what he needed. Once the two teachers understood each other's practices and came to a mutual agreement on the needs of individual children and the purpose of each teaching practice, the synergy was electric. As a team, the teachers decided together to place a few highly desirable works out of reach so the student would need to make a verbal request to access them.

> If ever a child asks why another child seems to be receiving special privileges because of a disability, our teachers will often reply, "In this class, we all get what we need." This answer seems to suffice in matters of fairness, dignity, and respect.

Montessori is an essential element of inclusion. It teaches *independence* and (with its emphasis on community, incorporating multi-age-grouped classrooms with lessons that target needed concepts within developmental planes of childhood) it also teaches *interdependence*. A Montessori 3-year cycle allows for flexibility when a child is either behind or ahead of his developmental age. Our benchmarks add a little bit more allowance for students with special needs, and the flexibility of Montessori allows us to make even further adaptations.

Children can be pulled out to work with specialists as needed, but always with the intent that they will come back to the regular classroom. That is their home community. The Montessori method focuses not only on academics but social and emotional aspects. Inclusion cannot work without an understanding of both.

At Elizabeth Academy, enrollment processes are complicated, but balance is an essential element of inclusion, so ratios are important. We aim for a ratio that is reflective of disability in the population at large, which generally works out to 15–20% children with special needs and 80–85% "typical" children—congruent with what a child would experience in their neighborhood community. This is critical to a successful inclusive environment. If the ratios are off, classrooms can become overwhelmed, and inclusion, which is supposed to work for everyone, may serve no one.

Benchmarks and boundaries are necessary elements of inclusion. Sometimes conditional enrollment is necessary. For this reason, we have determined criteria that set boundaries for students we are not equipped to serve, and we have established benchmarks for children with special needs (they align with the planes of development for typical children, but have more flexibility). These benchmarks also set clear goals for students and teaching teams to ensure that children are progressing and ready to move to the next level, and benchmarks assist our teaching teams in targeting very specific areas of skill-building and support. Mandy relates:

> We have learned over time that sometimes students need an extra year (or even two if they have special needs) within a specific level before they are ready to advance to the next program level. However, students should not be "held" at a level that is more than 2 years behind their peers of the same age. Keeping students who need support with their same-age peers keeps expectations high, and students are motivated to meet those expectations. Our benchmarks support students in progressing through the program. Students want and need to feel as if they belong, and they need to be with their same-age peers. We have found that when students are "held back," we frequently see negative behaviors increase because social and emotional needs are being overlooked.

After we have done all we can to support children in meeting these benchmarks, if they are not met before transition to the next program level, we have to consider whether or not the child should continue to be enrolled at our school. It is our intent that all children get what they need to progress. Our educational program is unsurpassed, but there are areas in which we have limits. If a child is in deep need of either emotional (psychological) or physical (medical) care, we may feel a moral obligation to discontinue their enrollment and support them in finding a program that will better meet their needs. Lizzie shares an experience that helped us realize the need to set these boundaries and how to deal with departures when they are necessary:

> There are some children we struggled to serve. One returning sixth grader had been in many different schools and worked with multiple therapists to help her emotionally and socially. Her teacher from the previous year moved to another school and two new teachers came into the classroom to replace the one who had left.
>
> The child was upset by her teacher's departure, and this may have been a catalyst for her behavior over the next 2 months. She hit others, swore, blamed others for her actions, made friends and then instantly made enemies, and cried and cried about no one understanding her.
>
> We made a plan with her parents to see if we could get these incidents down. However, things continued to escalate, and the situation in the classroom worsened. We gently told the child's parents that we needed to help them find a new educational placement. Even though we knew this would be a hard transition for the family, we also tried to look at it as a success for their daughter. We knew that she needed something more than we could offer. A psychiatrist or possibly a psychologist appeared to be the best professional to help her succeed, and we didn't have this at our school. We gave her parents a list of resources, and they placed her in an inpatient facility where she received constant one-on-one therapy for her needs.
>
> Her departure prompted deep discussions in the Upper Elementary classroom. We gathered in a circle on the rug. I explained that their classmate was not coming back to the school because her parents chose a better place to help her work through the challenges she faced each day. Then I called on children to share their feelings. Children who had been hurt both emotionally and physically by this girl said things like:
>
> "Even though she really hurt my feelings, I forgive her."
>
> "My dad says that when kids bully, it means they are having a hard time. I think this is what was happening with her. I hope she feels better soon."

"She was the first person to introduce me to others and give me a tour of the classroom. She was always kind to me."

"I am happy she will get the help she needs to be a better friend."

The Secondary School (2017–2019)

Lauren (on the right) laughing, smiling and having fun with her friends.

In the fall of 2017, we launched our secondary program with our first small group of ninth grade "high schoolers" and our seventh and eighth grade middle school students. This would be our most tremendous challenge yet. We re-evaluated leadership, learning, and resources and clearly identified what our program needed. These five areas of focus are described below.

Accreditation was a must. National accreditation would not only provide our high school students with credible transcripts and diplomas, but it would strengthen the whole school community. We had started this process with AdvancED when we opened the secondary school in 2017, but our efforts became much more earnest as we entered the second year.

The accreditation process required an in-depth evaluation of our systems and programs. All stakeholder groups (parents, students, teachers, community and board members) shed important light on areas of needed focus and improvement. Becoming nationally accredited required us to align our program with state requirements for graduation, meet accreditation standards related to our leadership, learning, and resource capacities, and develop a system for continuous improvement. National accreditation shows that our inclusive Montessori program meets industry standards for education. This also enabled us to offer transcripts that are fully recognized by other schools and postsecondary programs, something that is critical as our students start to think about life after graduation from high school.

Social and academic inclusion: In our current model, practitioners work and support all children so that in the children's eyes they are just teachers, and no one feels stigmatized for having "special needs." The idea is always to make the learning, adaptations, and support feel as natural as possible. What has evolved is a program that includes in-class and consultative support from speech-language pathologists, music therapists, occupational therapists, and physical therapists who work as a team with the classroom teachers to provide *all* students with the support they need.

The arts program has expanded at Elizabeth Academy and it is having a particular impact on inclusion, particularly at the Upper Elementary and Secondary levels. In the Secondary program we are integrating art therapy and sensorial art experiences into the core curriculum, making adaptations in the lessons and creating class projects utilizing various art forms. Art integration allows abstract concepts to be experienced concretely and sensorially, which deepens understanding. Our integrated art electives create by-products that fuel our micro-economy program, with lessons learned in electives that are crossing over and translating into mini businesses. For example, a culinary class informs the lunch program and is transforming the cafeteria into a lunch cafe, with students learning how to take and track orders, collect money, and serve the meals.

School-wide collaboration creates an inclusive element that aligns all levels and elevates each individual. Our teams have worked hard to become strong collaborators. Collaboration between therapists and teachers is critical, but so too is parental input and involvement. If goals are different between home and school, it confuses children, and they progress at a slower pace. Consistency between home and school is paramount.

Academic adaptations can be made utilizing apps, online resources, and the latest technologies that make a huge difference in the lives of students with special needs, as well as typical and gifted students. The beauty of Montessori is that the spiral curriculum allows for adaptability and the method lends itself to these integrated services in a natural way. Here is a personal example of how this worked for Lauren:

> Students in the Secondary program were assigned books to read. Lauren's group was assigned Bram Stoker's *Dracula*. Those in her group who could read the original manuscript did so. At 15 years old,

Lauren is reading, but it is still a struggle for her. She was given an edited version, but still needed a great deal of support. I was given an outline to work with her that would guide Lauren in understanding important elements of the story (character, themes, etc.), and she also worked privately with our Academic Adaptations specialist, Kelsi Bailey, who tutored Lauren using reading and writing apps (Learning Ally, Google Read and Write) and also employed visuals from *Dracula* movies to increase Lauren's comprehension of the text and story. This was all communicated to me, as her parent, so that I could also work with Lauren at home. I cannot believe the progress Lauren made in her reading comprehension, writing abilities, oral expression, and social/emotional maturity as these teachers engaged in this intensive, intelligent collaboration. As proof of Lauren's expanded vocabulary through reading *Dracula*, we were out shopping one day and a certain necklace caught her eye. "I want a CRUCIFIX!" she said. I looked to see what caught her eye—a stylized silver and turquoise cross dangling from a pebbled chain. ("Crucifix" was one of her vocabulary words from the book.) I'm not Catholic and I don't believe in vampires, but I bought that necklace for Lauren because I believe in the people, processes, and power of inclusive collaboration that I see working at Elizabeth Academy.

Montessori materials and work can be adapted to meet the needs of children with varying abilities, regardless of their age. Here Lauren works with the bead frames as a teenager, improving her math skills. Typically developing children may move on from this work before their teenage years.

A secondary student plays drums during music therapy lesson.

Secondary students enjoy the rich experience of creating art and benefit developmentally from the therapeutic value.

The Future—Colleges and Communities (2019–Beyond)

When I began my journey with Lauren to find the path that would lead her to a "normal" life of independent living, I realized that *no one* lives a completely independent life. As human beings, we are all interdependent. And that's the beauty of life. Sadly, I have also come to understand that because of Lauren's disability, she will always require more support than the average person throughout her entire life.

One in three families is affected by disability. Inclusion, therefore, is a pervasive human need. We simply must innovate with new educational paradigms to address this need. And we can't stop there. Life goes on after formal education ends. We need inclusive structures in our whole society. Inclusive Montessori is the perfect model for life.

Interdependence is an indispensable value to embrace on the path to our ultimate mission, which is replication. Broader collaboration outside our school community is the next step.

When we clashed with the district preschool as we began our journey, we learned an invaluable lesson about the need to respect other educational modalities and align wherever possible. We have now come full circle and are ready and able to collaborate with district schools. Through these partnerships, dual enrollment with local district high schools and concurrent enrollment with local colleges are possibilities. This will allow students more opportunities; they can take specialty coursework or participate in team sports and other activities we do not offer at Elizabeth Academy. The circle of inclusion widens as the students mature. Our next focus will be to create whole inclusive communities, starting with inclusive college housing and expanding to inclusive living communities.

A New Dawn

When Lauren emerged, bearing her tiny gift of Down syndrome, she illuminated the way for others to follow her, "the child," on a better educational journey. Inclusive Montessori is the way. This past holiday season, Lizzie gave me a little book with a gilded cover, knowing I would be drawn to the handwritten inscription just inside the cover. It read:

> If a man neglects education, he walks lame to the end of his life. —Plato

Education is for everyone. Without it we are all lame. And we are lame when we neglect the lame, whether that be a child with a physical or mental disability, or an adult who is weak in a teaching practice, or anyone else who is just plain difficult to work with. With inclusion, we all help each other walk a little faster, and a great deal taller, than we ever do alone.

Elizabeth Academy began with a tiny awakening. Every immense and worthy endeavor does. Awakenings in the heart enlighten the mind. Inclusion can happen. A new dawn of education is on the horizon.

Diversity is being invited to the party; inclusion is being asked to dance. ~Verna Myers

REFERENCES

Preface

Danner, N. (2015). Early childhood inclusion in a public Montessori school: Access, participation, and supports (Doctoral dissertation, University of Illinois at Urbana-Champaign).

Danner, N., & Fowler, S. (2015). Montessori and non-Montessori early childhood teachers' attitudes towards inclusion and access. Journal of Montessori Research, 1(1), 28–41.

Epstein, A. M. (1996). Teacher accommodation for individual differences in integrated Montessori early childhood classrooms (Doctoral dissertation). Retrieved from ProQuest Dissertations and Theses. (Accession No. 9707595)

Orem, R. C. (1969). Montessori and the special child. Putnam.

University of Kansas, Circle of Inclusion Project. (2016). Circle of inclusion. Retrieved from http://www.circleofinclusion.org/index.html

Chapter 1: Better Together: Montessori & Special Education

Adcock, M.W. (1990). Special education. In K. Kahn, J. Miller, & J. Bailis (Eds.), *Implementing Montessori education in the public sector* (pp. 272–283). Montessori Public School Consortium.

Arthaud, T. J., Aram, R. J., Breck, S. E., Doelling, J. E. & Bushrow, K. M. (2007). Developing collaboration skills in pre-service teachers: A partnership between general and special education. *Teacher Education & Special Education, 30*(1), 1–12.

Bouck, E. C. (2004). State of curriculum for secondary students with mild mental retardation. *Education & Training in Developmental Disabilities, 39*(2), 169–176. Retrieved from EBSCOhost.

Cahill, S. M., & Mitra, S. (2008). Forging collaborative relationships to meet the demands of inclusion. *Kappa Delta Pi Record, 44*(4), 149–151.

Cossentino, J. (2009). Culture, craft & coherence: The unexpected vitality of Montessori teacher training. *Journal of Teacher Education, 60*(5), 520–527. doi: 10.1177/0022487109344593

Cossentino, J. (2010). Following all the children: Early intervention and Montessori. *Montessori Life*, 22(4), 38–45. Retrieved from https://www.publicmontessori.org/wp-content/uploads/2016/10/Following-All-the-Children-Early Intervention-and-Montessori.pdf

Danner, N. & Fowler, S. A. (2015). Montessori and non-Montessori early childhood teachers' attitudes toward inclusion and access. *Journal of Montessori Research*, 1(1), 1–14. Retrieved from https://eric.ed.gov/contentdelivery/servlet/ERICServlet?accno=EJ1161287

Donabella, M. A., & Rule, A. C. (2008). Four seventh grade students who qualify for academic intervention services in mathematics learning multi-digit multiplication with the Montessori Checkerboard. *Teaching Exceptional Children Plus*, 4(3), 2–28. Retrieved from http://escholarship.bc.edu/education/tecplus/vol4/iss3/art2

Dubovoy, S. C. (2018). Is Montessori for every child in 2018? *Montessori Public*, 2(2), 1, 14–15. Retrieved from https://www.montessoripublic.org/2018/02/montessoripublic-print-edition volume-2-3-sped-ell/

Eccleston, S. T. (2010). Successful collaboration: Four essential traits of effective special education specialists. *Journal of The International Association of Special Education*, 11(1), 40–47.

Epstein, A. (1994). Special education: Is Montessori right for my child? *Public School Montessorian*, 6(4), 8–9.

Family Educational Rights and Privacy Act of 1974 (FERPA), 20 U.S.C. § 1232g; 34 CFR Part 99 (1974). Retrieved from https://www2.ed.gov/policy/gen/guid/fpco/ferpa/index.html

Gillies, R. M. (2014). Collaborative engagement: A key construct for the successful delivery of programmes and services for children and youth with special education needs. *International Journal of Disability, Development & Education*, 61(4), 327–331.

Gitter, L. L. (1967). The promise of Montessori for special education. *Journal of Special Education*, 2(1), 5–13.

Griffin, C. C., Kilgore, K. L., Winn, J. A., & Otis-Wilborn, A. (2008). First-year special educators' relationships with their general education colleagues. *Teacher Education Quarterly*, 35(1), 141–157.

Grskovic, J. A., & Trzcinka, S. M. (2011). Essential standards for preparing secondary content teachers to effectively teacher students with mild disabilities in included settings. *American Secondary Education*, *39*(2), 94–106. Retrieved from EBSCOhost.

Karvonen, M., Test, D. W., Wood, W. M., Browder, D., & Algozzine, B. (2004). Putting self-determination into practice. *Exceptional Children*, *71*(1), 23–41. Retrieved from EBSCOhost.

Leelanau Montessori. (2018). *The Staff at Leelanau Montessori Public School Academy*. Leelanau Montessori Public School Academy. Retrieved from http://www.leelanaumontessori.org/ourstaff.html

Leigh-Doyle, P., Maughan, J., & Joyce, M. (2008). Whole-school approaches to Montessori special education. *The NAMTA Journal, 33*(2), 147–176.

Lingo, A. S., Barton-Arwood, S. M., & Jolivette, K. (2011). Teachers working together. *Teaching Exceptional Children, 43*(3), 6–13.

Malone, D., & Gallagher, P. A. (2010). Special education teachers' attitudes and perceptions of teamwork. *Remedial and Special Education, 31*(5), 330–342.

McKenzie, G., & Zascavage, V. S. (2012). Montessori instruction: A model for inclusion in early childhood classrooms and beyond. *Montessori Life*, *24*(1), 32–38.

Montessori, M. (1912). *The Montessori method* (2nd ed). Frederick A. Stokes Company.

Morse, T. E. (2010). New Orleans's unique school reform effort and its potential implications for special education. *Education and Urban Society, 42*(2), 168–181. doi:10.1177/0013124509349570

Morton, M., & McMenamin, T. (2011). Learning together: Collaboration to develop curriculum assessment that promotes belonging. *Support for Learning*, *26*(3), 109–114. Retrieved from EBSCOhost.

Musanti, S. I., & Pence, L. (2010). Collaboration and teacher development: Unpacking resistance, constructing knowledge, and navigating identities. *Teacher Education Quarterly, 37*(1), 73–89.

National Center for Education Statistics. (2016). *Digest of education statistics*. Retrieved from https://nces.ed.gov/programs/digest/d16/tables/dt16_204.30.asp

National Center for Montessori in the Public Sector (NCMPS). (2018). American Montessori Society. Retrieved from http://www.public-montessori.org/

Nichols, S., & Sheffield, A. N. (2014). Is there an elephant in the room? Considerations that administrators tend to forget when facilitating inclusive practices among general and special education teachers. *National Forum of Applied Educational Research Journal, 27*(1/2), 31–44.

Shaker, N., & Abou-Zleikha, M. (2014). Alone we can do so little, together we can do so much: A combinatorial approach for generating game content. *Proceedings of the Tenth Annual AAAI Conference on Artificial Intelligence and Interactive Digital Entertainment,* 167–173. Retrieved from https://www.aaai.org/ocs/index.php/AIIDE/AIIDE14/paper/view/9000

Taylor, L. (2018). Montessori for all at Cornerstone: Welcoming specialists into high fidelity Montessori. *Montessori Public, 2*(2/3), 15–17. Retrieved from https://www.montessoripublic.org/2018/02/montessoripublic-print-edition volume-2-3-sped-ell/

Vas, N. (2008). The special needs child from the Montessori perspective. *The NAMTA Journal, 33*(2), 3–23.

Suggested Resources

American Montessori Society. (2015). *Montessori terminology.* Retrieved from http://amshq.org/Family-Resources/Montessori-Terminology

Alquraini, T. A. (2013). An analysis of legal issues relating to the least restrictive environment standards. *Journal of Research in Special Educational Needs, 13*(2), 152–158). doi: 10.1111/j.1471-3802.2011.01220.x.\

The Council for Disability Rights. (n.d.). *A parent's guide to special ed/special needs.* Retrieved from http://www.disabilityrights.org/glossary.htm

Loiacono, V., & Allen, B. (2008). Are special education teachers prepared to teach the increasing number of students diagnosed with autism? *International Journal of Special Education, 23*(2), 120–127. Retrieved from https://files.eric.ed.gov/fulltext/EJ814449.pdf

Montessori Commons. (2015). *Observation* (2015). Retrieved from http://montessoricommons.cc/observation/

Obiakor, F. E., Harris, M., Mutua, K., Rotatori, A., & Algozzine, B. (2012). Making inclusion work in general education classrooms. *Education and treatment of children, 35,* (3), 477–490. Retrieved from http://www.chowardbostic.com/articles/Obiakor%202012.pdf

Understanding Special Education. (2009). *Special education terms and definitions.* Retrieved from http://www.understandingspecialeducation.com/specialeducation-terms.html

Chapter 2: What New (and Not So New) Montessori Teachers Need to Know About Special Education

Archer, D. (2014, May 14). ADHD: The entrepreneur's superpower. *Forbes.* Retrieved from http://www.forbes.com/sites/dalearcher/2014

Armstrong, T. (n.d.). *The story of attention deficit disorder.* Retrieved from http://www.institute4learning.com/add-adhd_strategies.php

AuCoin, D., & Berger, B. (2015, March). *Successful passage for students with special needs from traditional school to Montessori schools –Montessori special education terminology* (workshop activity). American Montessori Society National Conference, Philadelphia, PA.

Awes, A. (2012). Supporting the dyslexic child in the Montessori environment. *Communications, 2012/1–2,* 54–75.

Barkley, R. A. (n.d.). *Fact sheet: Attention deficit hyperactivity disorder.* Retrieved from http://www.russellbarkley.org/factsheets/adhd-facts.pdf

Cossentino, J. (2009). Culture, craft & coherence: The unexpected vitality of Montessori teacher training. *Journal of Teacher Education, 60*(5), 520–527. doi: 10.1177/0022487109344593

Cossentino, J. (2010). Following all the children: Early intervention and Montessori. *Montessori Life, 22*(4), 38–45.

Council for Exceptional Children. (2012). *Initial and advanced standards for the preparation of special educators (Revised).* Retrieved from https://www.cec.sped.org/Standards/Special-Education-Professional-Preparation

Council for Exceptional Children (n.d.). *CEC's standards development process.* Retrieved from https://www.cec.sped.org/Standards/Standards-Development

Engelfried, G. (2018). Special needs parents have needs of their own. *Montessori Public, 2*(2), 9. Retrieved from https://www.montessoripublic.org/2018/02/montessoripublic-print-edition, volume-2-3-sped-ell

Friend, M., & Cook, L. (2007). *Interactions: Collaboration skills for school professionals* (5th edition). Allyn and Bacon.

Goertz, D. B. (2001). *Children who are not yet peaceful*. Frog Books.

Hughes, S. H. (2009). Montessori education, neuropsychology, and the child with special needs: Referral, assessment, and intervention. *The NAMTA Journal, 34*(2), 75–140.

Individuals with Disabilities Education Act of 2004 (IDEA), 20 U.S.C. § 1400 (2004).

Jones, A., & Cossentino, J. (2017). What's going on with this child? Child study for the 21st century. *The NAMTA Journal, 42*(2), 249–260.

Kahn, B. (2009a). Tutoring without crutches: Extra support and inclusion for the older Montessori child with learning differences. *The NAMTA Journal, 34*(2), 39–54.

Kahn, B. (2009b). 2009 NAMTA baseline special education survey. *The NAMTA Journal, 34*(2), 181–196.

Kramer, R. (1988). *Maria Montessori: A biography*. Addison-Wesley Publishing Company, Inc.

Lane, K. M. (2009). *Autism: A Montessori approach*. MLMAS.

Lillard, A. S. (2017). *Montessori: The science behind the genius* (3rd Edition). Oxford University Press.

McFarland, S. (1993). *Shining through: A teachers' handbook on transformation*. Shining Mountains Press.

McKenzie, G. K., & Zascavage, V. S. (2012). Montessori instruction: A model for inclusion in early childhood classrooms and beyond. *Montessori Life, 24*(1), 32–38.

Medscape. (2009, Oct 8). *Exercise and ADD: An expert interview with John J. Ratey, MD*. Retrieved from http://www.medscape.com/viewarticle/709864

Montessori, M. (2007). *The advanced Montessori method I: Spontaneous activity in education.* Montessori-Pierson Publishing Company. (Original work published 1917)

Montessori, M. (1995). *The absorbent mind.* Henry Holt and Company, LLC. (Original work published 1949)

Montessori, M. (1967). *The discovery of the child.* Ballantine Books, Inc. (Original work published 1909)

Montessori, M. (1969). Montessori lectures on special education. In Orem, R. C. (Ed.), *Montessori and the special child* (pp. 201–209). G. P. Putnam's Sons.

Montessori, M. (1971). *The four planes of education.* (M. Montessori, Ed.) Association Montessori Internationale.

Montessori, M. M. (1956). *The human tendencies and Montessori education.* Association Montessori Internationale.

Murray, A., & Peyton, V. (2008). Public Montessori elementary schools: a delicate balance. *Montessori Life, 20*(4), 26–30.

National Center for Education Statistics (NCES), U. S. Department of Education, Washington, D. C. (2018). *Digest of Education Statistics 2018, table 204.30.* Retrieved from https://nces.ed.gov/programs/digest/d18/tables/dt18_204.30.asp

National Center for Montessori in the Public Sector Staff. (2019, Winter). The Montessori Census speaks. *MontessoriPublic.org, 4*(3), 12.

Noddings, A. (2017a). Supporting sensory-sensitive children in a sensory-insensitive world. *Montessori Life, 29*(1), 35–39.

Noddings, A. (2017b). Classroom solutions for sensory-sensitive students. *Montessori Life, 29*(2), 45–49.

Noddings, A. (2017c). When sensory sensitivity requires intervention: Assessment and treatment of sensory-sensitive children. *Montessori Life, 29*(3), 39–43.

Pickering, J. S. (2017). Montessori for children with learning differences. *Montessori Life, 29*(1), 49–53.

Pickering, J. S. (2019). *Montessori strategies for children with learning differences: The MACAR model.* Parent Child Press, a division of Montessori Services.

Shanks, P. (2009). Inclusion: A preparation for life. *The NAMTA Journal, 34*(2), 241–252.

Shanks, P. (2014). Building the inclusive Montessori school. *The NAMTA Journal, 39*(3), 5–38.

Smith, D. D., Tyler, N. C., & Skow, K.G. (2018). *Introduction to contemporary special education: New horizons* (2nd ed.). Pearson Education, Inc.

Suggested Resources

Recommended books focusing on learning and behavioral challenges:

Ensher, G.E., & Clark, D.A. (2016). *The early years: Foundations for best practice with special children and their families.* Zero to Three.

Kaiser, B., & Rasminsky, J. S. (2017). *Challenging behavior in young children: Understanding, preventing, and responding effectively* (4th ed.). Pearson.

Pickering, J. S. (2019). *Montessori strategies for children with learning differences: The MACAR model.* Parent Child Press, a division of Montessori Services.

Smith, D. D., Tyler, N. C., & Skow, K. G. (2018). *Introduction to contemporary special education: New horizons* (2nd ed.). Pearson.

Recommended websites focusing on learning and behavioral challenges:

Collaborative and Proactive Solutions (Ross Greene): www.livesinthebalance.org

International Dyslexia Association: https://dyslexiaida.org/

Intervention Central: www.interventioncentral.org

IRIS Center at Vanderbilt University: https://iris.peabody.vanderbilt.edu/

LDonline.org: http://www.ldonline.org/index.php

National Center for Learning Disabilities: http://www.ncld.org/

National Center for Montessori in the Public Sector: http://www.public-montessori.org/

PBIS World: www.pbisworld.com

Reading Rockets: http://www.readingrockets.org/

Understood.org: https://www.understood.org

Zero to Three: https://www.zerotothree.org/

Recommended videos focusing on high-incidence disabilities:

ADHD/Executive Function

Center on the Developing Child at Harvard University (2012, June 18). *In brief: Executive function: Skills for life and learning* [Video file]. Retrieved from www.youtube.com/watch?v=efCq_vHUMqs

Autism Spectrum Disorders

ABA in PA Initiative (2016, February 18). *What is ABA therapy?* [Video file]. Retrieved from https://www.youtube.com/watch?v=GC968hBJGz8

Camden Council (2014, September 5). *The Teacch approach* [Video file]. Retrieved from https://www.youtube.com/watch?v=vkymZzmg4jw

CNN (2014, January 28). *What it feels like to be autistic* [Video file]. Retrieved from https://www.youtube.com/watch?v=1qPFAT4p8Lc

Iris Center (2014). *Autism spectrum disorder: An overview for educators* [Video file]. Retrieved from https://iris.peabody.vanderbilt.edu/module/asd1/

Kennedy Krieger Institute (2013, June 11). *Bringing the early signs of autism spectrum disorders into focus* [Video file]. Retrieved from: https://youtu.be/YtvP5A5OHpU

Public Broadcasting System 39 (2014, December 1). *Autism: Floortime therapy model* [Video file]. Retrieved from www.youtube.com/watch?v=gNAS9PskgYI

Emotional and Behavioral Disorders

Greene, R. (2010, September 10). *Kids do well if they can* [Video file]. Retrieved from https://www.bing.com/videos/

Chapter 3: Following All the Children: A Montessori Model of Tiered Instruction

Balu, R., Zhu, P., Doolittle, F., Schiller, E., Jenkins, J., & Gersten, R. (2015). *Evaluation of response to intervention practices for elementary school reading. NCEE 2016-4000.* National Center for Education Evaluation and Regional Assistance.

Brown, J. S. & Duguid, P. (1991). Organizational learning and communities-of-practice: Toward a unified view of working, learning and innovation. *Organization Science, 2*(1).

Committee to Evaluate the Supplemental Security Income Disability Program for Children with Mental Disorders; Board on the Health of Select Populations; Board on Children, Youth, and Families; Institute of Medicine; Division of Behavioral and Social Sciences and Education; The National Academies of Sciences, Engineering, and Medicine (2015, Oct 28). Poverty and childhood disability. In Boat, T. F., & Wu, J. T. (Eds.), *Mental disorders and disabilities among low-income children.* National Academies Press. Retrieved from https://www.ncbi.nlm.nih.gov/books/NBK332898/

Cossentino, J. (2009). Culture, craft & coherence: The unexpected vitality of Montessori teacher training. *Journal of Teacher Education, 60*(5), 520–527. doi: 10.1177/0022487109344593

Cossentino, J. (2005). Ritualizing expertise: A non-Montessori view of the Montessori method. *American Journal of Education, 111*(2), 211–244.

Cummings, K. D., Atkins, T., Allison, R. & Cole, C. (2008). Response to intervention: Investigating the new role of special educators. *Teaching Exceptional Children, 40*(4), 24–31.

Fuchs, D., & Fuchs, L. S. (2006). Introduction to response to intervention: What, why, and how valid is it? *Reading Research Quarterly, 41*(1), 93–99.

DuFour, R. (2004). Schools as learning communities. *Educational Leadership, 61*(8), 6–11.

Gitter, L. (1965). *A strategy for fighting the war on poverty (The Montessori method as applied to the Brookhaven Project).* Homer Fagan Press.

Gresham, F. M. (2002). Response to Treatment. In Bradley, R., Danielson, L., & Hallahan, D., *Identification of learning disabilities: Research to practice.* USED.

Hunt, J. M. (1961). *Intelligence and experience.* Ronald Press.

Lillard, A. S. (2017). *Montessori: The science behind the genius.* Oxford University Press.

McFarland, J., Hussar, B., Zhang, J., Wang, X., Wang, K., Hein, S., Diliberti, M., Forrest Cataldi, E., Bullock Mann, F., & Barmer, A. (2019). *The condition of education 2019 (NCES 2019-144).* U.S. Department of Education, National Center for Education Statistics. Retrieved October 9, 2019, from https://nces.ed.gov/pubsearch/pubsinfo.asp?pubid=2019144

Miller, B., Taylor, K., & Ryder, R. E. (2019). Introduction to special topic: Serving children with disabilities within multitiered systems of support. *AERA Open.* doi: 10.1177/2332858419853796

Montessori, M. (1988). *The absorbent mind.* Clio Press. (Original work published 1949)

National Council on Disability (2002). *IDEA reauthorization: Where do we really stand?* Retrieved from https://ncd.gov/publications/2002/July52002

Pickering, J. S. (2003). Montessori and learning differences. *Montessori Life, 15*(4).

Pickering, J. S. (2001). *The match teacher checklist: Observation of behavioral and academic performance in the Montessori classroom.* June Shelton School and Evaluation Center.

Rief, S. F. (2008). *The ADHD checklist: A practical reference of parents and teachers.* Jossey-Bass.

Rose, E. (2010). *The promise of preschool: From Head Start to universal pre-kindergarten.* Oxford University Press.

Snyder, T. D. (2016). *Mobile digest of education statistics 2014.* United States Department of Education, National Center for Education Statistics. Retrieved from http://nces.ed.gov/pubs2016/2016011.pdf

Schifter, L. A., Grindal, T., Schwartz, G., & Hehir, T. (2019). *Students from low-income families and special education.* The Century Foundation.

Tilly, W. D. (2008). The evolution of school psychology to science-based practice. In A. Thomas & J. Grimes (Eds.), *Best practices in school psychology V* (pp. 17–36). National Association of School Psychologists.

Wenger, E. (1998). *Communities of practice: Learning, meaning, and identity.* Cambridge University Press.

Whitescarver, K., & Cossentino, J. (2008). *Montessori and the mainstream: A century of reform on the margins*. Teachers College Record *110*(12), 2571–2600.

Chapter 4: An Overview of a Montessori-Based Multi-Tiered System of Support

Elliott, S. (2008). The effect of teachers' attitude toward inclusion on the practice and success levels of children with and without disabilities in physical education. *International Journal of Special Education 23*(4), 48–55. Retrieved from https://eric.ed.gov/?id=EJ833682

Inclusive Schools Network. (2015, June 10). *Together we learn better: Inclusive schools benefit all children*. Retrieved from inclusiveschools.org: inclusiveschools.org/together-we-learn-better-inclusive-schools-benefit-all-children/

National Center for Education Statistics. (2019, May). *Children and youth with disabilities*. Retrieved from_nces.ed.gov/programs/coe/indicator_cgg.asp

Rosen, P. (n.d.). *MTSS: What you need to know*. Retrieved from understood.org/en/learning-thinking-differences/treatments-approaches/educationalstrategies/mtss-what-you-need-to-know

Ross-Hill, R. (2009, November 18). Teacher attitude toward inclusion practices and special needs students. *Journal of Research in Special Educational Needs 9*(3), 188–198. doi: 10.1111/j.1471-3802.2009.01135.x?q=Ross+Greene%2c+video&view=detail&mid=E251BFBE341F5276466EE251BFBE341F5276466E&FORM=VIRE

Regional Intervention Program.org (2011, June 27). *Parenting that works 2011* [Video file]. Retrieved from https://www.youtube.com/watch?time_continue=3&v=PrIWJeGJuuM

Intellectual Disabilities

UpsDownsCalgary (2013, April 29). *Inclusion works: A resource for parents and educators about down syndrome* [Video file]. Retrieved from https://www.youtube.com/watch?v=3UzCn2WCUE8

Sensory Processing

Easter Seals Goodwill Northern Rocky Mountain (ESGWNRM) (2012, July 5). *A child's view of sensory processing disorder* [Video file]. Retrieved from https://www.bing.com/videos/h?q=Sensory+Processing+disorder%2c+video&&view=detail&mid=0C317139CB91284E0AF10C317139CB91284E0AF1&&FORM=VDRVRV

Speech and Communication Impairments

Akron Children's Hospital (2009, February 23). *Childhood speech and language delays* [Video file]. Retrieved from https://www.bing.com/videos/h?q=Language+development%2c+youtube&&view=detail&mid=3170215274B0415C27A53170215274B0415C27A5&&FORM=VDRVRV

The Stuttering Foundation (2011, October 12). *Stuttering: Straight talk for teachers* [Video file]. Retrieved from www.youtube.com/watch?v=ix65403ruKI

Solomon, A. (2012, December 11). *Andrew Solomon on deafness (FAR FROM THE TREE Chapter 2)* [Video file]. Retrieved from https://www.youtube.com/watch?v=VWhz3NWkjlk

Twice Exceptional

Aurora Public Schools (2018, June 4). *Twice exceptional students* [Video file]. Retrieved from https://www.youtube.com/watch?v=WYVJS5oVae8

Chapter 5: Supporting Children with Exceptionalities in an Independent Montessori School

Batsche, G. (n.d.). *Developing a plan*. Retrieved from http://www.rtinetwork.org/getstarted/develop/developingplan

Epstein, P. (2012). *An observer's notebook*. Learning from children with the observation C.O.R.E. (2nd Edition). The Montessori Foundation Press.

Epstein, P. (2001). Montessori moments. *Tomorrow's Child, 9*(5), 26–29.

Fisher, D. & Frey, N. (2010). *Enhancing RTI: How to ensure success with effective classroom instruction & intervention.* ASCD.

Fountas, I. C., & Pinnell, G. S. (n.d.). *Benchmark assessment system (BAS)*. Retrieved from http://www.heinemann.com/fountasandpinnell/BAS2_Overview.aspx

Harlacher, J. E., Sanford, A., & Walker, N. N. (n.d.). *Distinguishing between tier 2 and tier 3 instruction in order to support implementation of RTI*. Retrieved from http://www.rtinetwork.org/essential/tieredinstruction/tier3/distinguishing-between-tier-2-and-tier-3-instruction-in-order-to-support-implementation-of-rti

Johnson, E., & Pesky, L. (n.d.). *How to develop an effective tier 2 system*. Retrieved from http://www.rtinetwork.org/essential/tieredinstruction/tier2/how-to-develop-an-effective-tier-2-system

Lillard, A. S. (2005). *Montessori: The science behind the genius*. Oxford University Press.

N.W.E.A. (n.d.). *Measures of academic progress*. Retrieved from https://www.nwea.org/

Metcalf, T. (n.d.). *What's your plan? Accurate decision making within a multi-tier system of supports: Critical areas in tier 2*. Retrieved from http://www.rtinetwork.org/essential/tieredinstruction/tier2/whats-your-plan-accurate-decision-making-within-a-multi-tier-system-of-supports-critical-areas-in-tier-2

Montessori, M. (1991). *The advanced Montessori method-1*. (F. Simmonds, Trans.). Clio Press. (Original work published 1917)

Nellis, L. M. (2007). *Response-to-intervention: An overview and connection to other education initiatives*. Retrieved from http://www.slideshare.net/datacenters/response-to-intervention-power-point-revised?src=related_normal&rel=2656815

RTI Action Network. (n.d.). *What is RTI?* Retrieved from http://www.rtinetwork.org/learn/what/whatisrti

Seldin. T., & Epstein, P. (2003). *The Montessori way*. The Montessori Foundation Press.

VanDerHeyden, A. (n.d.). *Approaches to RTI*. Retrieved from http://rtinetwork.org/learn/what/approaches-to-rti

Wiggins, G., & McTighe, J. (2005). *Understanding by design (expanded 2nd edition)*. ASCD.

Chapter 6: How Can I Tell Her Parents?

Montessori, M. (2005). *A decalogue*. Association Montessori Internationale. Retrieved from http://www.alternative-montessori.com/wp-content/uploads/2012/09/Decalogue.pdf

Chapter 7: Montessori Teacher Supports for Children with Exceptionalities

American Academy of Pediatrics (n.d.). *Developmental milestones: 3- to 4-year-olds*. Retrieved from https://www.healthychildren.org/English/ages-stages/toddler/Pages/Developmental-Milestones-3-to-4-Years-Old.aspx

Association Montessori Internationale (n.d.). *AMI Montessori and the common core state standards*. Retrieved from https://amiusa.org/ami-montessori-and-the-common-core-state-standards/

Berk, L. E., & Winsler, A. (1995). *Scaffolding children's learning: Vygotsky and early childhood education*. National Association for the Education of Young Children.

Center for Disease Control (n.d.). *CDC's developmental milestones*. Retrieved from https://www.cdc.gov/ncbddd/actearly/milestones/index.html

de la Riva, S., & Ryan, T. G. (2015). Effect of self-regulating behavior on young children's academic success. *International Journal of Early Childhood Special Education, 7*(1), 69-96.

Common Core Standards Initiative (n.d.). *Read the standards*. Retrieved from http://www.corestandards.org/read-the-standards

Gourley, L., Wind, C., Henninger, E. M., & Chinitz, S. (2013). Sensory processing difficulties, behavioral problems, and parental stress in a clinical population of young children. *Journal of Child and Family Studies, 22*, 912–922.

Gray, C. (2004). Social Stories™ 10.0 The new defining criteria & guidelines. *Jennison Autism Journal, 15*(4), 2–21.

Hartlep, K. L., & Forsyth, G. A. (2000). The effect of self-reference on learning and retention. *Teaching of Psychology, 27*(4), 269–271.

Individuals with Disabilities Education Act of 2004 (IDEA), 20 U.S.C. § 1400 (2004).

Lillard, P. (1972). *Montessori: A modern approach*. Schocken Books.

Luborsky, B. (2017). Helping children with attentional challenges in a Montessori classroom: The role of the occupational therapist. *The NAMTA Journal, 42*(2), 287–352.

Montessori, M. (1964). *The Montessori method*. Schocken Books, Inc. (Original work published 1909)

Montessori, M. (1965). *Dr. Montessori's own handbook: A short guide to her ideas and materials*. Schocken Books, Inc. (Original work published 1914)

Montessori, M. (1966). *The secret of childhood*. Ballantine Books. (Original work published 1936)

Montessori, M. (1967). *The discovery of the child*. Ballantine Books. (Original work published 1909)

National Center for Montessori Education in the Public Sector (n.d.). *The common core state standards*. Retrieved from https://www.public-montessori.org/resources/montessori-in-the-public-sector/the-common-core-state-standards/

Noddings, A. (2017). Classroom solutions for sensory-sensitive students. *Montessori Life, 29*(2), 45–49.

Sensory Processing Disorder (n.d.). Retrieved from https://www.sensory-processing-disorder.com/

Sweet, M. (2010). Helping children with sensory processing disorders: The role of occupational therapy. *Odyssey*, Spring/Summer 2010, 19–22.

U.S. Department of Education, National Center for Education Statistics. (2015). *Digest of Education Statistics, 2013* (NCES 2015-011), Table 204.30. Retrieved from http://nces.ed.gov/fastfacts/display.asp?id=64

Chapter 8: Montessori as a Safe Haven for Childhood Trauma

Centers for Disease Control and Prevention (n.d). *About the CDC-Kaiser ACE study*. Retrieved from https://www.cdc.gov/violenceprevention/childabuseandneglect/acestudy/about.html

Bloom, S. L. (2012). Trauma-organized systems. In C. R. Figley, *Encyclopedia of trauma* (pp. 741–743). SAGE Publishing.

Felitti, V.J., Anda, R.F., Nordenberg, D., Williamson, D.F., Spitz, A.M., Edwards, V., Koss, M.P., & Marks, J.S. (1998). Relationship of childhood abuse and household dysfunction to many of the leading cause of deaths in adults: The Adverse Childhood Experiences (ACE) study. *American Journal of Preventive Medicine, 14*(4), 245–258.

Franco, F. (2018). Childhood abuse, complex trauma and epigenetics. *Psych Central*. Retrieved November 2, 2019, from https://psychcentral.com/lib/childhood-abuse-complex-trauma-and-epigenetics/

Montessori, M. (1967). *The absorbent mind*. Holt, Rinehart and Winston. (Original work published 1949)

National Child Traumatic Stress Network (NCTSN). (n.d.). *Defining trauma and child traumatic stress*. Retrieved September 14, 2019, from http://www.nctsnet.org/nccts/nav.do?pid=faq_def

Perry, B., & Szalavitz, M. (2007). *The boy who was raised as a dog: And other stories from a child psychiatrist's notebook—What traumatized children can teach us about*. Basic Books.

Perry, B. (2016, December 14). The brain science behind trauma. *Education Week, 36*(15), 28.

Sackett, G. (2016). The scientist in the classroom: The Montessori teacher as scientist. *The NAMTA Journal, 41*(2), 1–20.

Sar, V. (2011). Developmental trauma, complex PTSD, and the current proposal of DSM-5. *European Journal of Psychotraumatology, 2*. doi:10.3402/ejpt.v2i0.5622

van der Kolk, B. (2015). *The body keeps the score: Brain, mind, and body in the healing of trauma*. Penguin Books.

Chapter 9: Trauma-Informed Montessori

Bowlby, J. (1969). *Attachment and loss: Vol. 1. Attachment*. Basic Books.

Montessori, M. (1982). *The secret of childhood*. Ballantine Books, p. 149. (Original work published 1936)

Szalavitz, M., & Perry, B. (2011). *Born for love: Why empathy is essential—and endangered*. William Morrow Publishers.

Chapter 10: Including Young Children with Severe Disabilities in Raintree Montessori School: The Circle of Inclusion

Avramidis E., & Norwich, B. (2002). Teachers' attitudes towards integration/inclusion: A review of the literature. *European Journal of Special Needs Education, 17*(2), 129–147. doi: org/10.1080/08856250210129056

Axtell, S. A. M., Garwick, A. W., Patterson, J., Bennett, F. C., & Blum, R. W. (1995). Unmet service needs of families of young children with chronic illnesses and disabilities. *Journal of Family and Economic Issues, 16,* 395–411. Retrieved from https://link.springer.com/article/10.1007%2FBF02353690

Bailey, D. B., Blasco, P. M., & Simeonsson, R. J. (1992). Needs expressed by mothers and fathers of young children with disabilities. *American Journal on Mental Retardation, 97,* 1–10. Retrieved from https://www.researchgate.net/publication/21768452_Bailey_D_B_Jr_Blasco_P_M_Simeonsson_R_J_Needs_expressed_by_mothers_and_fathers_of_young_children_with_disabilities_American_Journal_of_Mental_Retardation_971_1-10

Baumgart. D., Brown, L., Pumpian, I., Nisbet, J., Ford, A., Sweet, M., Messina, R., & Schroeder, J. (1982). Principle of partial participation and individualized adaptation in educational programs for severely handicapped students. *Journal of the Association for the Severely Handicapped, 7*(20), 17–27.

Berk, H. J., & Berk, M. L. (1982). A survey of day care centers and their services for handicapped children. *Child Care Quarterly, 11*(3), 211–214. Retrieved from https://link.springer.com/article/10.1007%2FBF01115554?LI=true

Booth-LaForce, C., & Kelly, J. F. (2004). Childcare patterns and issues for families of preschool children with disabilities. *Infants and Young Children, 17*(1), 5–16. Retrieved from https://depts.washington.edu/isei/iyc/laforce_17_1.pdf

Brooke, T. (1992). *A comparison of an integrated setting versus a special education setting using the CEVIT (coding environmental variables and interactions on tape)* (Unpublished master's thesis). University of Kansas, Lawrence, KS.

Buysse, V., & Bailey, D. (1993). Behavioral and developmental outcomes in young children with disabilities in integrated and segregated settings: A review of comparative studies. *Journal of Special Education, 26*(4), 434–461. doi: 10.1177/002246699302600407

Cannella, H. I., O'Reilly, M. F., & Lancioni, G. E. (2005). Choice and preference assessment research with people with severe to profound developmental disabilities: A review of the literature. *Research in Developmental Disabilities, 26*(1), 1–15. doi:10.1016/j.ridd.2004.01.006

Diamond, K. E., Hestenes, E. S., Carpenter, E. S., & Innes, F. K. (1997). Relationships between enrollment in an inclusive class and preschool children's ideas about people with disabilities. *Topics in Early Childhood Special Education, 17*(4), 520–536. doi: 10.1177/027112149701700409

Dunn, W. (1997). The impact of sensory processing abilities on the daily lives of young children and families: A conceptual model. *Infants & Young Children, 9*(4), 23–35. Retrieved from http://img2.timg.co.il/forums/71501742.pdf

Guralnick, M. (1990). Major accomplishments and future directions in early childhood mainstreaming. *Topics in Early Childhood Special Education, 10*(2), 11–7. doi: 10.1177/027112149001000202

Gitter, L. L. (1967). The promise of Montessori for special education. *The Journal of Special Education, 2*(1), 5–13. doi: 10.1177/002246696700200101

Gitter, L. L. (1971). *The Montessori approach to special education.* Mafex Associates, Inc.

Grisham-Brown J., & Hemmeter, M. L. (2017). *Blended practices for teaching young children in inclusive settings* (2nd edition). Brookes Publishing Co.

Hanline, M. F. (1993). Inclusion of preschoolers with profound disabilities: An analysis of children's interaction. *Journal of the Association for Persons with Severe Handicaps (JASH), 18*(1), 28–35. doi: 10.1177/154079699301800105

Horn, E., Palmer, S., Butera, G., & Lieber, J. (2016). *Six steps to inclusive preschool curriculum: A UDL-based framework for children's school success.* Brookes Publishing Co.

Horn, E., & Kang, J. (2012). Supporting young children with multiple disabilities: What do we know and what do we still need to learn? *Topics in Early Childhood Special Education, 31*(4), 241–248. doi: 10.1177/0271121411426487

Horn, E., Thompson, B., & Nelson, C. (2004). Implementing inclusion across the grade levels: Collaborative teams. In C. Kennedy & E. Horn, *Including students with significant disabilities: Putting research into practice*. Brookes Publishing Co.

Horn, E., Thompson, B., Palmer, S., Jenson, R., & Turbiville, V. (2004). Implementing inclusion across the grade levels: Preschool. In C. Kennedy & E. Horn, *Including students with significant disabilities: Putting research into practice*. Brookes Publishing Co.

Jenkins, J. R., Odom, S. L., & Speltz, M. L. (1989). Effects of social integration of preschool children with handicaps. *Exceptional Children, 55*, 420–428. doi: 10.1177/001440298905500505

Klein, N., & Sheehan, R. (1987). Staff development: A key issue in meeting the needs of young handicapped children in day care settings. *Topics in Early Childhood Special Education, 7*(1), 13–27. doi: 10.1177/027112148700700103

Kimura, L. (1991). *Reliability analysis for environmental variables of the CEVIT (coding environmental variables and interactions on tape): A tool for observing young children with severe multiple disabilities in an integrated Montessori school* (Unpublished master's thesis). University of Kansas, Lawrence, KS.

Krogh, S. (1981). Moral beginnings: The just community in Montessori preschools. *Journal of Moral Education, 11*(1), 41–46. doi: 10.1080/0305724810110104

Krogh, S. (1982). Affective and social development: Some ideas from Montessori's prepared environment. *Topics in Early Childhood Special Education 2*(1), 55–62. doi: 10.1177/027112148200200110

Leon, D. (1992). *Reliability analysis for interaction variables of the CEVIT (coding environmental variables and interactions on tape): A tool for observing young children with severe multiple disabilities in an integrated Montessori school.* (Unpublished master's thesis). University of Kansas, Lawrence, KS.

Lit, T. L. (1993). *A comparison of integration facilitators of young children with severe disabilities in an inclusive preschool setting* (Unpublished master's thesis). University of Kansas, Lawrence, KS.

McLean, M., & Hanline, M. F. (1990). Providing early intervention services in integrated environments: Challenges and opportunities for the future. *Topics in Early Childhood Special Education, 10*(2), 62–77. doi: 10.1177/027112149001000206

Montessori, M. (1965). *Dr. Montessori's own handbook.* Schocken Books. (Original work published 1914)

Montessori, M. (1973). *From childhood to adolescence* (A. M. Joosten, Trans.). Schocken Books. (Original work published 1948)

Montessori, M. (1967). *The absorbent mind* (C. Claremont, Trans.). Dell Publishing. (Original work published 1949)

Montessori, M. (1983). *The secret of childhood* (B. B. Carter, Trans.). Sangam Books. (Original work published 1936)

Noonan, M. J., & McCormick, L. (2014). *Teaching young children with disabilities in natural settings (2nd edition).* Brookes Publishing Co.

Orem, R. C. (1969). *Montessori and the special child.* G. P. Putman's Sons.

Rice, M. L., & O'Brien, M. (1993, December). *Kansas early childhood research institute on transitions: Final report.* Kansas Early Childhood Research Institute. Retrieved from https://archive.org/stream/ERIC_ED376641/ERIC_ED376641

Sandall, S. R., & Schwartz, I. S. (2008). *Building blocks for teaching preschoolers with special needs (2nd edition).* Brookes Publishing Co.

Shanks, P. (1990). *Rediscovering the potential in a children's house: A handbook for persons facilitating the integration of young children with severe disabilities in a Montessori environment* (Unpublished master's thesis). University of Kansas, Lawrence, KS.

Shanks, P. (2009). Inclusion: A preparation for life. *The NAMTA Journal, 34*(2), 241–252.

Stargardter, S. (1988). *Staff and parents' perceptions about the integration of children with severe and multiple disabilities into a community preschool program.* (Unpublished master's thesis). University of Kansas, Lawrence, KS.

Stegemann, A. (1993). *A re-analysis of videotaped segments of three young children with severe disabilities in two preschool environments* (Unpublished master's thesis). University of Kansas, Lawrence, KS.

Thompson, B., & Guess, D. (1989). Students with the most profound multiply handicapping conditions: Teacher perceptions. In F. Brown & D. Lehr (Eds.), *Persons with profound disabilities: Issues and practices* (pp. 3–43). Brookes Publishing Co.

Thompson, B., & Wegner, J. (Exec. producers/directors) (1992). *The circle of inclusion (Educational video and manual)*. Learner Managed Designs, Inc.

Thompson, B., & Wegner, J. (Exec. producers/directors) (1992). *The process of communication: Facilitating interactions with young children with severe disabilities in mainstream early childhood inclusion (Educational video and manual)*. Learner Managed Designs, Inc.

Thompson, B., Wickham, D., Mulligan Ault, M., Shanks, P., Reinertson, B., Wegner, J., et al. (1991). Expanding the circle of inclusion: Integrating young children with severe multiple disabilities. *Montessori Life* (Winter), 11–14.

Thompson, B., Wickham, D., Wegner, J., Ault, M., Shanks, P., & Reinertson, B. (1993). *Handbook for the inclusion of young children with severe disabilities: Strategies for implementing exemplary full inclusion programs*. Learner Managed Designs, Inc.

Thompson, B., Wickham, D., Wegner, J., & Ault, M. (1996). All children should know joy: Inclusive, family-centered services for young children with significant disabilities. In D. H. Lehr & F. Brown, (Eds.), *People with disabilities who challenge the system* (pp. 23–55). Brookes Publishing Co.

Wegner, J. (1991). *From classroom to classroom: New ways to interact* (Unpublished doctoral dissertation). University of Kansas, Lawrence, KS.

Chapter 11: Elizabeth Academy: Awakening to a New Dawn

Montessori, M. (2005). *Dr. Montessori's own handbook*. Dover Publications, Inc., pp. 107–123. (Original work published 1914)

KSL TV [Elizabeth Academy]. (2013, April 25). *Elizabeth Academy opens its doors in 2009*. Retrieved from https://www.youtube.com/watch?v=oVjFAkPm4IM.

ACKNOWLEDGMENTS

I am very grateful to each of our authors. Several began drafting chapters in 2016 and continued refining their work through 2020. Several joined us later and met very short deadlines with grace and insight.

Madie Sherman, my University of Wisconsin—La Crosse undergraduate researcher, cheerfully took on every task with amazing skill.

Carey Jones, our copy editor, not only found just the right words for every chapter but kept us on track, meeting after meeting.

Thank you to the schools and individuals who contributed photos of children actively engaged in inclusive classrooms.

Publishers Joe Campbell and Jane Campbell are extraordinary individuals. They embraced our stories and strategies with open hearts and deep appreciation for children with exceptionalities and their teachers.

And thank you to every teacher, administrator, and family member who embraces Montessori as an inclusive, joyful learning adventure for all children.

Ann Epstein, PhD
Primary Editor